This Book Belongs to
Jean Mann

Secrets of Happiness

Bob & Debby Gass

Secrets of Happiness

Bridge-Logos *Publishers* Gainesville, Florida 32614 USA

Secrets of Happiness

by Bob & Debby Gass

Copyright © 2000 by Bob Gass
Library of Congress Catalog Card Number: Pending
International Standard Book Number: 0-88270-840-6

Published by:

Bridge-Logos *Publishers*

PO Box 141630
Gainesville, FL 32614

To

_____

From

_____

Date

_____

Introduction

A successful life is made up of successful choices. Here are seven you need to consider.

1.   Chose love: No occasion or excuse justifies hatred.
2.   Chose joy: Since God is directing your steps, resist the temptation to be negative or cynical.
3.   Chose patience: Instead of cursing the one who takes your place, step aside and invite him in. Instead of complaining that the wait is too long, thank God for a moment to pray.
4.   Chose kindness: Be kind to the poor, for often they are alone. Be kind to the rich, for often they are afraid. Be kind to the unkind, then you'll understand how God deals with you.
5.   Chose goodness: Be quicker to confess than to accuse, to be overlooked than to boast, and to go without than to accept that which is dishonest.
6.   Chose faithfulness: Keep your promises so that your creditors will never regret their trust, nor your friends question your word, nor your family doubt your love and commitment.
7.   Chose gentleness: Nothing is won by force. If you raise your voice, let it be in praise. If you clench your fist, let it be in prayer. If you make a demand, let it first be on yourself.

These seven choices are all based on one thing – character – and that's what this book is all about!

Table of Contents

Preface

The Bible lists nine qualities that make up character and calls them "The fruit of the spirit." They are love, joy, peace, patience, kindness, goodness, faithfulness, gentleness and self-control.

One translation of the Bible names the nine character traits as being: (1) Affection for others, (2) Exuberance about life, (3) Serenity, (4) A willingness to stick with things, (5) A sense of compassion in the heart, (6) A conviction that a basic holiness permeates things and people, (7) We find ourselves involved in loyal commitments, (8) Not needing to force our way in life, and (9) We are able to marshal and direct our energies wisely (Galatians 5:22-23 TM).

Fruit takes time to grow. It must be planted, watered, fertilized, and protected, if it is going to develop on a tree or in your life. You can try to lift yourself by your own bootstraps to produce these things through human effort, but Jesus said, "I am the vine; you are the branches. If a man remains in me and I in him, he will bear much fruit. Apart from me you can do nothing." (John 15:5 NIV).

You become like the company you keep. As you spend time with God in prayer and in His Word, these character traits will grow automatically.

As you look at these nine lessons in character, you will discover that you are strong in some areas and weak in others. Don't be discouraged. Life is a marathon, not a one-hundred-yard dash. Furthermore, since today is the first day of the rest of your life, it is never too late to start.

If you want to grow, you will. All you need is the commitment to say, "I want the character of Christ to be seen in me."

Now let's take a closer look at each of these Christ-like characteristics.

Chapter One

Affection For Others

Appreciation

Helen Morsla, a teaching nun, tells of the day her kids were fighting in class. So she made them each take a piece of paper, list the names of all the other students - and write something they liked about each of them. Then she wrote the name of each student at the top of a fresh sheet of paper, listed all the nice things the other students had said about them, and gave it to them. As they read them in amazement, they each said, "I never knew they felt that way!"

Helen moved away, but years later when she came home on vacation, her Dad said to her, "The Ecklands called last night to say their son Mark was killed in Vietnam, and they'd like you to come to the funeral." After the service, Mark's former classmates gathered in the family home, including Helen, their old teacher. Suddenly Mark's dad said to her, "I'd like to show you something, I found it in my son's wallet." Opening a billfold, he removed a familiar sheet of paper that was now yellow and worn - listing all the good things each of his classmates had said about him. Then one by one, smiling sheepishly, all the others opened their purses and billfolds too and produced theirs. Helen said, "All I could do was just sit down and cry."

What would make a boy carry a fifteen-year-old piece of paper everywhere he went, even to his death in a rice patty half way around the world? The answer is appreciation! There are people all around you today who are hungry and hurting for appreciation. Make sure you give it to them.

The Power of Love

Tommy had a particularly hard time in school. He constantly asked questions and was never able to keep up. His teacher finally gave up on him, told his mother that he couldn't learn, and said that he would never amount to much. But Tommy's mother was a nurturer; she believed in him. She taught him at home, and each time he failed, she gave him hope and encouraged him to keep trying.

Whatever happened to Tommy? Well, eventually he grew up and became an inventor, holding more than 1,000 patents, including the phonograph and the first electric light bulb. You guessed it - his name was Thomas Edison. When people have love and hope, there's no telling how far they can go!

Solomon said, "Pleasant words are... healing..." (Pr 16:24). Words either build up or tear down. How do people feel when they're around you? Do they feel small and insignificant, or do they believe in themselves and begin to realize what they can become?

The Bible is a book of hope. It tells us Jonah got a second chance to go back to Nineveh (Jonah 3:1); the prodigal son came back from a wasted life and was restored to his family (Luke 15:11); and Peter, the man who denied the Lord, became the leader of the church. Today, ask God to make you an encourager, a nurturer, and a restorer.

Do it Anyway

When Bishop Able Muzore was asked to lead the African National Counsel, he prayed as he had never prayed before. Most of his predecessors had been killed or imprisoned, so he struggled with this decision, until a friend handed him these life-changing words:

"People are unreasonable, illogical and self-centered - love them anyway! If you do good, they'll accuse you of selfishness or ulterior motives - do good anyway! When you're successful, your friends may be false, and your enemies will be real - succeed anyway. The good you do today may soon be forgotten tomorrow - do well anyway! Honesty and frankness will make you vulnerable - be honest and frank anyway! The biggest people with the biggest ideas can be shot down by the smallest people with the smallest minds - think big anyway! People favor underdogs but only follow top dogs - fight for the underdog anyway! What you spend years building may be destroyed overnight - build anyway! Give the world the best you've got, and the chances are, you'll still be despised - give your best anyway!"

How is such a lifestyle possible? You are to "Let every detail of your lives - words, actions, whatever - be done in the name of the Master, Jesus, thanking God... every step of the way" (Colossians 3:17 TM). Now that's the way to live!

Encouragement

There are enough critics in the world; what we need are more cheerleaders. If you want to get the best out of people, start doing these 4 things:

1. Appreciate them for who they are. Look at children; they blossom under praise, and wilt under constant criticism. Teenagers today are committing suicide in increasing numbers because they feel they never measure up! If you only feel loved when you do well instead of being valued for who you are, life becomes a "no-win situation."

2. Anticipate the best from them. Forget what they are at the minute, and help them to see what they can be in the future. Encourage them to stretch. Raise your anticipation level, and you'll raise their achievement level. That's how it works!

3. Admire their accomplishments. Instead of always pointing out their failures, help them to build on their successes. John Maxwell says, "Man does not live by bread alone; sometimes he needs a little buttering up." He's right!

4. Accept your personal responsibility. Coach Bear Bryant, who led his team all the way to the Super Bowl, says, "There are 3 things I tell my players: If it goes bad - I did it. If it goes semi-good - we did it. If it goes real good - they did it." That's what it takes to make a winner! Today ask God to make you an encourager of others.

Giving Back

Eugene Lang stands in the elementary school in Harlem, where he graduated 53 years ago. Looking over an audience of twelve year olds in their caps and gowns, he says, "This is your first graduation - just the perfect time to dream! Decide what you want to be, and never let go of your dream!" He continues, "If you'll work hard and stay in school I'll...." Then he pauses dramatically, and as if inspired he announces, "I'll give each of you a college scholarship!" Suddenly a wave of emotion breaks as parents jump to their feet cheering, weeping and hugging each other. In a community where 90% of the children drop out of school, a Puerto Rican child runs into her mother's arms shouting, "I'm going to college! I'm going to college!" It's a scene of ecstasy!

In his 70's, Eugene Lang has come back to his "roots", and brought his "I Have A Dream Foundation" with him. He's here to give back what has been given to him. Other businessmen have caught his vision too, and they're going into schools all over New York, doing the same thing. All these children needed was somebody to believe in them, and their lives were changed forever. The most miserable people on earth, are those who wonder how the world is going to make them happy. The happiest people, are those who've invested their lives into others. That's why Jesus is saying to you and me today, "Freely ye have received, freely give."

Working With Others

When you meet people today who need encouragement, go ahead and give it to them, for more people die of broken hearts than swelled heads. Recently, a little boy was wanting to play darts with his father. He said, "Come on Dad, let's play darts. I'll throw, and you shout 'wonderful!'"

You may smile, but we tend to become what the most important people in our lives think of us. So think the best, believe the best, and express the best toward them - for your words will help to shape their destiny.

Remember that change takes time! Even though change seems simple, it is rarely ever easy. The only way we can break old habits is to form new ones - and that takes time, lots of time! You can't tell people something once and expect them to do it. They've got to hear it over and over again before they can make the adjustment.

Be persistent! Never give up trying to help them improve! Express gratitude for every inch of progress they make. Flying off the handle doesn't help one bit. The only way to get lasting results is through patience and persistence. Remember, "...Love always hopes, always perseveres... never fails..." (1Co 13:7-8 NIV). Ask God to give you that kind of love today.

For The Sake Of Your Children

The story goes like this: "One day my husband and I got into an argument and ended up yelling at each other. I retreated to the porch and sat with my head in my hands, crying. Our two-year-old daughter overheard the argument. "I love you Mom," she said, as she sat beside me and put her arms around me. "I love you too," I said. She rested her head on my shoulder, hugging me hard. "I wish you could love my Daddy too," she said. Talk about ripping your heart out! "But I do love your Daddy. We just had a disagreement," I responded. With that my daughter smiled, got up, and walked away. "Where are you going?" I asked, to which she replied, "I'm going to tell Daddy you love him!"

If you expose your children to your anger, make sure they are around to see your forgiveness. Teach them how to deal with the issue - without attacking the person. Let them know that a difference of opinion can lead to a decision that makes things better for everyone, and also that you can be wrong and still be respected and loved.

That may mean teaching them what you were never taught. If so, learn from the mistakes of your parents and pass it on to your children. Forgive when you're hurt and don't take your resentments to bed. Jesus said you must forgive "...so that your Father in heaven may forgive you..." (Mk 11:25 NIV). So, do it for the sake of your children.

You Can't Keep It To Yourself

Fritz Kreisler, the world famous violinist, earned a fortune through his concerts, but he gave most of it away. Once when he discovered an exquisite violin, he wasn't able to buy it. Later, when he had the money, he found that it had already been sold to a collector.

So Kreisler went to plead for the violin, but the man said, "No, it is my prized possession." Disappointed, Kreisler said, "Before I leave, could I play it just once before it's consigned to silence?" The owner agreed, and the great virtuoso filled the room with such magnificent music that the collector was moved to tears. Deeply stirred he said, "I have no right to keep this to myself; it's yours, take it into the world and let people hear it." When God blesses you with something, remember that you have no right to keep it to yourself - you have to give it away!

Nothing lives in the Dead Sea because it takes water in, but doesn't give any out. The quickest way to die spiritually is to hoard your blessings and chase spiritual experiences from one place to another. God is looking for people He can trust with His blessing. People will arrive in heaven one day and say, "Lord, I've used up every penny, every hour, and every ounce of vision and energy you gave me - to bless others." They are the ones who will hear the words, "Well done, good and faithful servant" (Mt 25:23). Will you be one of them?

The Wall

Their wedding picture mocked them from the table, these two whose minds no longer touched each other. They lived with such a wide barricade between them that neither battering rams of words nor artilleries of touch could break it down. Somewhere between the oldest child's first tooth and the youngest daughter's graduation they lost each other. Throughout the years each slowly unraveled that tangled ball of string called self, and as they tugged at stubborn knots, each hid the searching from the other.

Sometimes she cried at night and begged the whispering darkness to tell her who she was. He lay beside her snoring like a hibernating bear, unaware of her winter. She took a course in modern art, trying to find herself in colors splashed on canvas, complaining to the other women about men who were insensitive. He climbed into a tomb called the office, wrapped his mind in a shroud of paper figures and buried himself in his customers.

Slowly the wall between them arose, cemented by the mortar of indifference. One day, while reaching out to touch each other, they found a barrier they could not penetrate. Recoiling from the coldness of the stone, each retreated from the stranger on the other side. For when love dies, it is not in a moment of angry battle or when fiery bodies lose their heat. No, it lies panting, exhausted, and expiring at the bottom of a wall it could not scale.

Being There

Sometimes wisdom whispers, "Just be quiet!" When his wife lost her mother, TD Jakes discovered that though he loved his wife deeply, there are some things we all must face alone. Only the Lord can sustain you and get you through those times. Human hands are not strong enough to carry you, and the truth is, there are some stages of grief that you are not supposed to be rescued from. It is a process that can't be aborted or rushed.

The fact is that "When they walk through the valley of weeping it will become a place of... blessing and refreshment... they will grow constantly in strength" (Ps 84:5-6 LB). You can't stay in this valley - but neither can you avoid it. If you're grieving the loss of a loved one, Jesus alone can speak with authority, for He is the only one who ever made an appointment beyond the grave - and kept it! That qualifies Him to be your deliverer, your comforter, and your healer.

After He had laid three sons in a grave, Joseph Bailey wrote, "I was sitting, torn by grief, when someone came and talked to me of God's dealings, of why it happened, of hope beyond the grave. He said things I knew were true, but I was unmoved. I wished he'd go away. He finally did. Then another came and sat beside me for an hour and more. He just listened when I said something, answered briefly, prayed simply, and left. I was moved. I was comforted. I hated to see him go." Sometimes just "being there" and letting God do the rest is the best thing you can do.

Putting Others First

Don't be like the boss who wrote a memo to the personnel director saying, "Search the company for an alert, talented young man who can step into my shoes, and when you find him - fire him!" You may smile, but if you feel constantly threatened by somebody else's success or need to blow their light out just to let yours shine, then you've got a problem you need to deal with. That problem is insecurity and jealousy, and it will rob you of God's best for your life.

When Hitler was looking for a chauffeur, he selected the shortest man he could find, and kept him as his driver for the rest of his life. This man was so short that he actually needed special blocks under the driver's seat just so he could see over the steering wheel. Hitler used other people to make himself look bigger than he really was. Do you do that?

Paul says, "Take delight in honoring each other" (Romans 12:10 LB). Whose life are you making a difference in today? Every person you meet has a seed of success inside him or her, but most can't find it. That's where you come in! Help them to find it, even if it means sacrificing yourself to do it. Look at their temperament, their desires, and their opportunities. Once you find that seed, fertilize it with encouragement and water it with opportunity. If you do, you'll have the joy of seeing that person blossom before your eyes. Everybody is assigned to somebody. Find out whom you've been assigned to, and pour your life into him or her.

Always Expect the Best

Arthur Gordon tells the story of a friend who belonged to a men's writing club comprised of several bright young writers. Each time they met, one of them would read his story and the others would critique it with such viciousness that eventually they called themselves "The Stranglers."

On the same campus, however, a group of women also formed a writer's group called "The Wranglers." But instead of showering criticism on each other, they spent their time trying to find positive, encouraging things to say to each other, no matter how weak or underdeveloped the writing was.

Twenty years later, not one of "The Stranglers" had made a name for himself as a writer. But "The Wranglers" produced six women, who gained national prominence as writers. One of them was Marjorie Kinnan Rawlings who later won a Pulitzer prize.

That story dramatically illustrates the power and importance of praise and positive input into the lives of others. For most people, it's not what they are that holds them back - it's what they think they're not! "The Stranglers" made one another feel unqualified to write, and in time they became convinced of it.

If only somebody in that group had taken the initiative to be positive and nurturing, maybe a Hemingway, a Faulkner, or a Fitzgerald would have emerged to give the world another library of masterpieces. Think about that!

Chapter Two

Exuberance About Life

Every Day is Special

These words by Anne Wells should make all of us sit up and think: "My brother-in-law opened the bottom drawer of my sister's bureau and lifted out a package. In it was an exquisite silk slip. The price tag was still attached. His wife, Jan, had bought it the first time she went to New York, about 8 or 9 years ago. She never wore it; she said she was saving it for a special occasion. Well, I guess this is the occasion.

He put the slip on the bed with the other clothes we were taking - to the funeral home. Suddenly he slammed the drawer shut, turned to me and said, 'Don't ever save anything for a special occasion. Every day you live is a special occasion!'

Those words changed my life; I'm not saving anything anymore. Now we use our good china and crystal for every special occasion – like losing a pound, getting the sink unstopped, or seeing the first camellia blossom. 'Some day' and 'One of these days' are losing their grip on my vocabulary. If it's worth seeing, hearing, or doing, I want to do it now! I'm trying very hard not to put off, hold back, or save anything that would add laughter or luster to our lives. Every morning when I open my eyes, I tell myself – "today is special."

Makes you think, doesn't it? Makes you want to drain the last ounce of joy out of every day and break free from the concrete of procrastination that whispers, "You can do it later." Take that trip! Wise-up; forgive that offense! Tell that person you love them! Go back to school! Decide now to do the thing you've been putting off, for today is that special day you've been waiting for.

You Can Make a Difference

"Most people are more capable and more important than me. Who am I anyway to think that I could make a difference?" Is that how you feel? If it is, just be glad that Henry Ford, Martin Luther King, Jr., Winston Churchill, Abraham Lincoln, and the Apostle Paul didn't think like you!

How many did it take to rescue the dying man on the Jericho Road? One good Samaritan. How many did it take to confront Pharaoh and lead the exodus? One man. In 1645, one vote gave Oliver Cromwell control of England. In 1776, one vote gave America the English language instead of German. In 1868, one vote saved President Andrew Jackson from impeachment. In 1941, one vote gave Adolph Hitler control of the Nazi party!

Esther, a Jewish girl, who was married to a pagan King, broke long-standing tradition, marched into her husband's throne room, spoke her mind, and rescued her nation from a holocaust. One woman – only one – saved the nation, because she was willing to get personally involved to the point of sacrifice and say, "If I perish, I perish" (Esther 4:16).

Before you say, "Somebody else should be doing this instead of me," read these words: "I am only one, but I'm still one. I cannot do everything – but I can do something. And because I cannot do everything, I will not refuse to do something that I can do." Ask God today, "What can I do in this situation?"

Being Classy

When others speak well of you, you have acceptance; but when the truth speaks well of you, you have class! Demetrius had it. Do you? Before you answer, listen to Paul's words to Timothy: "Set an example… in speech, in life, in love, in faith, and in purity… give yourself wholly to them, so that everyone may see your progress" (1 Ti 4:12-15 NIV). That's class!

Consider the attributes of class. Class is simply confidence dressed in humility. It keeps its word, its temper, and its friends. It has a steady eye, a steady nerve, a steady tongue, and steady habits. It's silent when it has nothing to say, thoughtful when it judges, and is always first to make amends when it's wrong. Class doesn't run scared. It's sure footed, committed, and handles whatever comes along. Class has a sense of humor. It knows that a good laugh is often the best lubricant for oiling the machinery of human relations.

Class never makes excuses. It takes its lumps, learns from its mistakes and becomes wiser. Class knows that courtesy and good manners are nothing more than a series of small sacrifices. It bespeaks an aristocracy that is not dependent on ancestors or money. A blue blood can be totally without it, while the son of a Welsh miner may ooze it out of every pore. Class can walk with kings, yet still keep its virtue - talk with crowds, yet still maintain the common touch. Everyone is comfortable with a person who has class – because they are comfortable with themselves! Choose to become a person of class.

An Attitude of Gratitude

Do you have an attitude of gratitude, or are you a constant complainer? It's so easy to forget your blessings. Paul says, "Give thanks in all circumstances, for this is God's will for you" (1 Th 5:18 NIV).

Here is a prayer you need to pray: "Even though I clutch my blanket and growl when the alarm goes off, thank you Lord that I can hear; there are many who are deaf. Even though I close my eyes as long as possible against the morning light, thank you Lord that I can see; there are many who are blind. Even though I huddle in my bed and put off the effort to rise, thank you Lord that I have the strength to get up; there are many who are bed-ridden. Even though the first hour of my day is hectic, when socks are lost, toast is burned and tempers are short, thank you Lord for my family; there are many who are all alone. Even though our breakfast table never looks like the pictures in the magazines and the menu at times is unbalanced, thank you Lord for the food we have; there are many who are hungry. Even though the routine of my job is sometimes monotonous, thank you Lord for the opportunity to work; there are many that have no job. Even though I complain from time to time and wish my circumstances were not so limited, thank you Lord for the gift of life – and 101 other blessings that I've taken for granted."

Love and Marriage

Anne Landers offers a definition of love and marriage that would be hard to improve upon:

"Love is friendship that has caught fire. It's quiet understanding… mutual confidence… sharing and forgiving. It's loyalty through good times and bad. It settles for less than perfection, and make allowances for human weakness. Love is content with the present, hopes for the future, and refuses to brood over the past. It's the day-in and day-out chronicle of irritations, problems, compromises, small disappointments, big victories, and working together toward common goals.

If you have love in your life, it can make up for a great many things that you lack. If you don't, no matter what else there is - it's not enough."

Then she adds, "If you want to make your marriage work, observe these five rules. (1) Never both be angry at once, and never yell – unless the house is on fire. (2) Yield to each other. If you have to choose between making yourself or your mate look good – choose your mate. (3) Neglect the whole world rather than each other, and never let a day end without saying at least one complimentary thing to the one you love. (4) Never meet without an affectionate welcome, and never go to bed mad. (5) When you make a mistake, talk it out and ask for forgiveness.

Since God thought up the whole idea of marriage in the first place, why don't you ask Him for help with yours today?

Be a Mentor

In 1919, a young man recovering from war injuries rented a small apartment in Chicago to be near the famous author, Sherwood Anderson, who had helped many young writers. They became friends and for several years shared meals, took walks, and discussed writing night after night. Although Anderson was brutally honest, the young novice would take notes, return to his typewriter, and improve his material. In 1926, the young man published his first novel, "The Sun Also Rises" and suddenly Ernest Hemingway's career was launched.

But there's more! Anderson moved to New Orleans, met another young man with a burning desire to write, and put him through the same process: critiquing, discussing, encouraging – and always more writing. Three years later this new talent, William Faulkner, produced "The Sound and the Fury," which became an American masterpiece.

And there's even more! Anderson spent his next years in California working with another aspiring young writer called John Steinbeck. All told, his students earned three Nobel Prizes and four Pulitzer Prizes. Why did he do it? Because Anderson had been mentored by Theodore Dreiser, who had himself sat under the great Carl Sandburg.

Are you getting the idea? Paul told Timothy to pass on to others what had been given to him. Don't be the last link in the chain; don't let it die with you! Live on by taking what God has given you, and depositing it into somebody else.

Come On, You Can Do Better

William Johnston, owner of the Ritz-Carlton Hotels, has a wonderful saying: "Quality is a race with no finish line"! Natalie Nabal writes, "If 99.9 percent is good enough, then every year the following tragedies would occur: two million documents would be lost by the IRS, 12 babies daily would be given to the wrong parents, 291 pacemaker operations would be performed incorrectly, 20,000 drug prescriptions would be wrongly written, and 114,500 mismatched pairs of shoes would be shipped." That may not mean much to you—unless it was your baby or your pacemaker!

Why are some Christians willing to accept a standard of work that wouldn't be accepted anywhere else? Just saying, "We're supposed to love everybody," does not excuse sloppiness. If Christ lives in us, shouldn't we excel and have an edge? David said, "How excellent is thy name in all the earth" (Ps 8:1). Did you get that? God wants anything that's done in His name to be done with excellence. To those who offered Him less, He said, "You dishonor my name with your actions" (Mal 1:12 NLT). How would you feel if Jesus had just paid 99.9 per cent of your sin debt?

Paul writes, "I keep working toward that day when I will finally be all that Christ… wants me to be" (Phlp 3:12 NLT). Come on – you can do better!

The Station

In his great essay, "The Station", Robert Hastings writes, "Tucked away in our sub-conscious, is an idyllic vision. We see ourselves on a long train trip that spans the continent. Out the windows we drink in the passing scenes — children waving, cattle grazing, rolling hillsides, city skylines and village halls. But uppermost in our minds is the final destination. On a certain day, we'll pull into the station, bands will play, and flags will wave. Once we arrive, so many wonderful dreams will come true, and the pieces of our lives will fit together like a completed jigsaw puzzle.

"Restlessly we pace the aisles, despising the minutes… waiting… waiting… waiting for the station. When we reach the station, 'That will be it,' we cry! 'When I'm 18!' 'When I buy my first Mercedes.' 'When I get married.' 'When I put my last child through college.' 'When I've paid off the mortgage.' 'When I get that promotion.' 'When I reach retirement.' Waiting… waiting… waiting for the station. But sooner or later we realize that the true joy of life is not the destination - but the journey itself!"

Heaven will come soon enough; in the meantime, David said, "This is the day which the Lord hath made; we will rejoice and be glad in it" (Ps 118:24). Stop pacing the aisles and counting the miles; life must be lived as you go along. The station will come soon enough!

Keep Growing

By the time most people are in their mid-thirties, they've stopped acquiring any new skills or new attitudes. Does that shock you? Stop and think; how long has it been since you acquired a new skill? How many new attitudes have you adopted in your home lately? Or on your job? Or in your spiritual walk? How bound are you to mechanical performance? Do you feel compelled to approach a problem the same way every time? Does a new idea make you put up your guard or retreat into your shell? Are you addicted to predictability?

Solomon says, "Above all and before all, do this – get wisdom!" (Pr 4:7 TM). Chuck Swindoll says, "Living and learning go hand in hand – just like existing and expiring. The same hours and minutes that capture the wonder of a child, deepen the rut of an adult. To them learning is natural; to some of us it's a nuisance." How tragic!

Remember Caleb? At eighty-five he was still growing, and grabbing the future (Jos 14:12). When he should have been in comfortable retirement, he was out fighting giants and claiming mountains. While his friends were yawning, he was yearning. Every time the sun came up, it was a new adventure for him.

God says, "Enlarge the place of your tent... do not hold back; lengthen your cords, strengthen your stakes (Isa.54:2 NIV). That's you He's talking to!

Just for Today

Read these words… slowly… carefully… and thoughtfully.

Just for today, I'll experience and enjoy each hour to the fullest and not try and tackle my whole life's problems all at once. Just for today, I'll try to improve my mind by learning more than I now know; I'll read something that requires effort, thought, concentration, and commitment. Just for today, I'll be agreeable, look my best, speak in a well-modulated voice, and be courteous and considerate to others. Just for today, I won't find fault or try to change or improve anyone – but myself. Just for today, I'll have a plan and a goal. I might not follow them exactly, but I'll have them nonetheless. By doing that, I'll save myself from two enemies – hurry and indecision! Just for today, I'll exercise my character. I'll do a good turn and keep it secret; if anyone finds out, it won't count. Just for today, I'll do something that I don't want to do, that way I'll teach my spirit to rule my flesh and my will to rule my emotions. Just for today, I won't be afraid to love or to risk; I'll dare to enjoy all God's blessings, and believe that every seed I sow in His Kingdom will be multiplied back to me a hundred times over!

That's how I'll live – just for today!

It's All In Your Attitude

Jerry's the kind of guy who is always in a good mood. When you ask him how he's doing, he replies, "If I were any better, I'd be twins!" When you question him about his attitude, he says, "Every morning I say to myself, 'Jerry, you've two choices today; you can be in a bad mood or a good one'; I always choose the good one. When something bad happens, I can choose to be a victim, or I can choose to learn from it; I choose to learn. When somebody comes to me complaining, I can accept their complaint, or I can point out what's positive; I choose what's positive."

One day Jerry was robbed, shot, and seriously injured. This is how he tells what happened: "As I lay wounded on the floor, I knew I'd two choices; I could choose to live, or I could choose to die; I chose to live. The paramedics were great; they told me I was going to be fine. But when they wheeled me into the emergency room and I saw the expression on the doctor's face, I really got scared. That look said, 'He's a dead man!' So I knew I had to take action. When the nurse asked me if I was allergic to anything I said, "Yes, bullets!" Over their laughter, I told the doctor - I choose to live. Operate as if I'm going to live, not die!"

Today, Jerry lives and blesses people wherever he goes. Three things saved him: God's grace, modern medicine, and an attitude of faith. You may not get to choose your circumstances, but every day you get to choose your attitude. Make sure you choose the right one today!

Come On – Get With It!

Howard Hendricks writes, "Recently I lost one of my best friends, a woman 86 years young. She was the most exciting lay-teacher I've ever been exposed to. The last time I saw her on planet earth was at one of those 'Christian parties' where we all sit on eggshells and try to look pious.

"In she walked, looked at me and said, 'Well Hendricks, I haven't seen you for a long time. Tell me, what's the five best books you've read in the last year?' (That'll change the group dynamics in a hurry). Her philosophy was, 'Let's not bore each other with each other; let's get into a discussion. And if we can't find anything to discuss, then let's get into an argument.'

"She was 83 on her last trip to the Holy Land. She went with a group of NFL football players. One of my most vivid memories of her, is seeing her out in front yelling back to them, 'Come on men, get with it!'

"Recently she died in her sleep in her daughter's home in Dallas. Her daughter told me that just before she died, she had written out her goals for the next 10 years!"

Wow! Whether you're 29 or 92, the words for you today are: make plans, walk with God, and live till your last breath!

Chapter Three

Serenity

One Who Stands Beside To Help

Recently I read about a man who underwent open-heart surgery. He said, "The day before my surgery, a lovely nurse came into my room to visit me. She took me by the hand and said, 'During the surgery tomorrow you'll be disconnected from you heart and kept alive by machines. When the operation is over you'll awaken in the recovery room, but you won't be able to move for about six hours. You won't be able to speak or even open your eyes, but you'll be perfectly conscious. You'll hear and know everything that's going on around you. That can be frightening, so during those hours I'll stay by your side and hold your hand, as I am right now. I'll be with you until you're fully recovered. If you become anxious or afraid, just feel the touch of my hand on yours, and know that you're not alone, for I won't leave you.'

"It happened exactly as she said. I awoke, and even though I could do nothing - just the touch of her hand on mine, made all the difference!"

What a picture! Jesus' favorite word for the Holy Spirit is "paraclete" which means "one who stands beside to help." Engrave those words on your mind today until they're such a part of you that regardless of what you're going through, you'll always know with certainty that God's Spirit is surrounding you, sustaining you, and strengthening you. You're His child and that's His promise to you!

Take Some Time Out

If the light on your inner dashboard is flashing red, you're probably carrying too much weight, moving too fast, in need of a tune-up, or out of fuel. If you don't pull over, you'll be sorry, and so will those who love you. But if you have the courage to pull over and make some changes, you'll be well rewarded. But be warned; there are three problems you'll face if you do.

First, you'll experience "false guilt." By saying "no" to the people you've always said "yes" to, you'll feel a twinge of guilt. Ignore it — it's false guilt! It's based on wrong thinking and screwed-up values. Re-tune your conscience to God's Word and the priorities of His Kingdom.

Second, you'll experience hostility and misunderstanding. Certain people won't understand your slower pace, especially those who are still in the sinking boat you just stepped out of. Stick to your guns. In time, those who matter most will see the wisdom of what you're doing. Hey, they may even follow you!

Third, you'll encounter some personal and painful insights. By not filling every spare moment with activity, you'll begin to see the real you - and you may not like some of what you see. (Business can be a great place to hide.) But if you stay with it, you'll turn the corner and be well on the road to a healthier, happier, freer, and more fulfilling life.

Your goal should be to fulfill your destiny, and in the process to stay in balance, in good health, and in God's will!

Feel The Fear And Do It Anyway

The Greek word for fear means "to flee from danger." When God says, "Fear not," He is really saying, "You can shake and you can sweat, but you can't run!"

Elizabeth Elliott, wife of one of the five missionaries murdered in Equador many years ago, says she was constantly controlled by fear. Every time she tried to step out to do something for God, fear stopped her. Sound familiar? Then one day a friend told her something that changed her life. She said, "Feel the fear - and do it anyway!" Those words set her free, and they'll set you free too.

God doesn't say "don't feel afraid." No, He says, "don't give in to it!" Any time you do something you've never done before, fear will rush in - that's normal. When it does, don't think you're unspiritual or weak. God said to Moses, "Fear not..." - because there was something to fear—Pharaoh and the Red Sea! But God's answer was: "Do not be afraid. Stand firm and you will see the deliverance the Lord will bring you today" (Ex 14:13 NIV).

It's ok to look at the obstacles and feel the fear, as long as you hear God saying, "I will be with you" (Jos 1:5). What has God put in your heart to do? If you're tired of holding back, then dig in your heels, set your face like a flint, feel the fear - and do it any way - and you'll have victory! Why? Because God is with you. What more do you need?

The Cure For Perfectionism

Have you ever met a perfectionist who was truly happy? Whenever things must always be a certain way, life can make you pretty miserable, simply because life constantly changes. Instead of being content and grateful for their blessings, perfectionists constantly focus on what is wrong, and the subsequent need to fix it. It could be a disorganized closet, a dent in their car, a job they did that was less than perfect, or a few pounds they'd like to lose.

Or it could be someone else's imperfections: the way they look, the way they behave, or the way they live their lives. The very fact that they constantly focus on imperfections makes it impossible for them to be thankful - and gratitude is basic to all happiness.

This has nothing to do with striving for excellence. Rather, it has to do with fixating on what's wrong with life. Sure, there's always a better way to do something, but that doesn't mean you can't enjoy life the way it is at the moment.

Catch yourself before you fall into your habit of insisting that things should be different than the way they are. Gently remind yourself that life is ok, and that - in the absence of your judgement - everything will be just fine. Why? Because God's in control! Start dealing with your need for perfection by developing an attitude of gratitude. Do it, and you'll begin to discover how wonderful life really is.

God's Protection

"Those who live in the shelter of the most high will find rest in the shadow of the almighty. This I declare of the Lord: He alone is my refuge, my place of safety; He is my God, and I am trusting Him, for He will rescue you from every trap and protect you from the fatal plague. He will shield you with His wings, He will shelter you with His feathers. His faithful promises are your armor and protection.

"Do not be afraid of the terrors of the night, nor the dangers of the day, nor dread the plague that stalks the darkness, nor the disaster that strikes at noonday. Though a thousand fall at your side, though ten thousand are dying around you, these evils will not touch you.

"If you make the Lord your refuge, if you make the most high your shelter, no evil will conquer you, no plague will come near your dwelling. For He orders His angels to protect you wherever you go. They will hold you with their hands to keep you from striking your foot on a stone.

"I will rescue those who love me. I will protect those who trust in my name. When they call on me, I will answer; I will be with them in trouble. I will rescue them and honor them. I will satisfy them with a long life and give them my salvation" (Psalm 91 NLT).

Now read it again and feel His arms around you; let His peace fill your heart.

Living With Loose Ends

God won't tell you what you don't need to know. He won't do for you what He's already told you to do. Stop trying to figure out things that should be left in His hands. When you put something on the shelf that is bothering you and say you're going to trust God with it, don't take it back because you don't like the way He's handling it, or the length of time He's taking to do it. The Word says, "He that believeth shall not make haste" (Isa 28:16). Paul says, "Do not be anxious about anything..." (Php 4:6 NIV). That's rough if you're insecure or a "make-it-happen" person.

Your mind likes to slot everything, right? It wants to find some place to put everything so that it seems to make sense and feel like it's "taken care of." It doesn't like unanswered questions. But one of the tools God uses to crucify your carnal mind is unanswered questions. When we don't know, we either trust God, worry, or try to figure it out ourselves.

God doesn't always give us answers to our questions because He is training us in trust. Let that sink in! Learn to live with loose ends and trust God! If you want growth, you've got to be at peace with the mess and the mistakes that accompany it. If you are one of God's compulsive-obsessive children who has to put everything in a neat little package, then this is what you need to hear: "Trust in the Lord with all your heart; do not depend on your own understanding" (Pr 3:5 NLT).

God's Love For You

You wouldn't be so critical of yourself, or so conscious of the opinions of others, if you really knew how God felt about you! He made up His mind about you before you ever failed; so repent and dismiss the guilt, for guilt is the offspring of unbelief, and that insults God's mercy. Stop running from place to place looking for love. Open your heart; God is speaking to you today in the very circumstances you're trying to escape. He's the one you need when life has wounded you and you've fallen from your nesting place like a bird. Only His hand can catch your falling soul, cast it to the wind, and give you strength to fly again.

The problem is that we've never been loved by anyone the way He loves us, so we've nothing to compare it to. Some of us have never been secure in the love of our natural parents, and it affects how we see our heavenly Father. Go back to His Word! Read it until you believe it! It's a living love letter to you. It's a "statement of intent" from a God who wants nothing but the best for you. But you say, "I fall so far short." Nothing you've done has changed His mind about you. His love remains - it's unconditional.

Good parents don't want their child to be insecure or to question their love. That's why God disciplines us, delivers us, and delights in us! The fact that He loves you even when you're wrong is what gives you the power to right the wrongs you've done. Why don't you come to Him today and experience His love afresh?

Happiness Is An Inside Job

William James said, "The greatest discovery of our generation is that we can alter our lives by altering our attitudes." Think about that! It's your thought life, not your circumstances, that determines your happiness.

We keep thinking that we'd be happy if only a certain thing would happen. For example, some mothers say, "When Johnny gets out of elementary school, I'll be happy." And they are for a while, but then they say, "When Johnny graduates from high school I'll be happy." And they are, at least for the summer. Next, Johnny's graduation brings the same promise, and so does his marriage, and the birth of the first grandchild. But the problem is, the mother hasn't learned how to be happy between "happenings"! If your happiness is always controlled by something outside yourself, you'll always be hostage to circumstances. That's not God's plan for you!

David said, "I will bless the Lord at all times: His praise shall continually be in my mouth" (Ps 34:1). David chose the right attitude and you've got to choose it too. You've also got to maintain it. That's the hard part. It's like the old farmer who said, "The hardest thing about milking cows is that they never stay milked!"

And it's the same with attitudes. They don't stay changed; you've got to work on them every day.

Grace Be Unto You

Things that conquer others won't conquer you - if you've been given the grace to handle them! How could Paul persevere through beatings, betrayals, shipwrecks and imprisonment? He wrote, "Then He told me, 'My grace is enough; it's all you need. My strength comes into its own in your weakness'" (2Co 12:9 TM). Grace will enable you to care for an aged loved one who requires much time and patience, pray and never let go of a prodigal son or daughter, pastor in a difficult area, or work with joy in a miserable environment.

When does grace come? When you need it most, as Hebrews 4:16 says, "And we will find grace to help us when we need it" (NLT). God will not give you tomorrow's grace today, but when you wake up in the morning, it will be there - grace equal to every need.

One of the greatest mistakes you can make is to envy someone else or try to be like them. Why? Because you may have equal talent, but unless you are equally graced, you won't succeed. Indeed, getting what they have could bury you instead of bless you.

How does grace come? Again, Paul wrote, "And now, brethren, I commend you to God, and to the word of His grace, which is able to build you up..." (Acts 20:32). There it is—in the pages of God's Word! You'll either find the solution, or the grace to handle it, learn from it, and come out stronger. Grace be unto you today!

Finding Peace

Recently I heard of a mother with three children who complained to her doctor, "I just can't get the house cleaned the way I like it before everyone leaves in the morning." She was so stressed-out about it that the doctor had to put her on anti-depressants. It was like she had a gun pointed at her head and a voice inside her that said, "Every dish must be put away and every towel folded - or else!" Life had become one big emergency, and she could never "catch up." Yet, nobody but her had created the stress she was experiencing. Sound familiar?

Have your goals become so all-consuming that you've forgotten how to have fun along the way, or to "cut yourself some slack?" Have you made your preferences a condition for your happiness? Do you beat yourself up when you can't meet your self-created deadlines?

The first step toward recovering your peace of mind is to admit that you are creating your own emergencies. Life will go on wonderfully even if it doesn't go according to your plan. Don't wait until you lose a marriage or have a heart attack before you find that out.

The cause of perfectionism is self-centeredness; the cure is gratitude and service. When you live for others, it takes the focus off you. When that happens, you become more enjoyable to be around, and you find real peace in the process. Imagine that!

Are You In The Fire Today?

If you could talk to the three Hebrew children about the fiery furnace, perhaps they'd describe their experience with the Lord this way:

"The fire was all over us. Our robes were ablaze, but amazingly, our skin was unaffected. We had no idea what was going on. Then something moved over in the ashes; we were not alone!

"Suddenly out of the smoke came a shinning, gleaming… person! We never got His name. He never said it. He never said anything in fact, but just knowing He was there brought comfort in the fire. His presence created protection in the midst of the crisis.

"Now, we don't mean that the fire went out. No, it still burned, but the brightness of the flames was eclipsed by the brilliance of His presence.

"We never saw Him again; He only showed up when we needed Him most. But one thing is sure, looking back, we're glad that they dragged us from the presence of the wicked king into the presence of the righteous King! For in His presence we learned that, 'No weapon that is formed against thee shall prosper'" (Isa 54:17).

Are you walking through the fire today? If you are, remember you're not alone – He's there with you! Take courage! When He brings you out you'll know Him much better, trust Him much more, and have something to say to others that's really worth sharing.

The "What Ifs"

Either you carry the burden, or you let the Lord carry it. The choice is yours! How does He sustain us? One day at a time. Remember the Israelites in the wilderness? God supernaturally fed them each day by sending manna from Heaven. But like us, some of them wanted to make sure they would also have enough for tomorrow (just in case God forgot, or changed His mind). But God would only allow them to collect enough for each day. If they tried to collect more - the excess rotted. Similarly, when you worry over the future, you're trying to store up manna for tomorrow, and before you know it, you feel rotten. Your heavenly Father wants you to give your tomorrow to Him because it's too big for you.

Are you being tormented by the "What ifs?" What if the money doesn't come? What if I get hurt, or seriously ill, or lose my job? What if I'm lonely all my life? What if I'm not hearing from God, and I make a big mistake? The Bible calls this "imaginations" (2 Co 10:4). You are literally imaging the worst. Paul says to, "cast it down," for if you don't, you'll live in dread concerning things that haven't even happened, and probably never will - unless you create them through fear.

You must relax! What if you reason and reason and figure it all out, then God surprises you and does something different? All that time would be wasted! Haven't you already wasted enough time worrying? Here's an idea: what if you just relax and let God be God?

Chapter Four

A Willingness to Stick With Things

Be Persistent

Jessie Owens set his first world record in junior high school. Then in college, he set three world records in less than an hour. In 1936, he showed his character at the Olympics in Nazi Germany. As Hitler watched, he broke three more world records, and won four gold medals. Losing to a black American was more than Hitler could stand that day, and he stormed out of the stadium in a rage.

Later Jessie Owens wrote: "There is something that can happen to every athlete and every human being; the instinct to slack off. To give in to pain, to give less than your best... the instinct to hope you can win through luck, or through your opponent not doing his best, instead of going to the limit and past your limit, where victory is always found. Defeating those negative instincts that are out to defeat us, is the difference between winning and losing - and we face that battle every day of our lives."

Persistence is based on character, and character does what's right - not what's easy. It's controlled by values - not moods. It looks for solutions - not excuses. Kipling wrote, "If you don't get what you want, it's a sign that either you didn't want it seriously enough, or that you tried to bargain over the price." How badly do you want to fulfil your purpose in life? It will take passion on your part to do it, and passion is what will feed your persistence. You must "run with perseverance the race marked out for you!"

Morning Comes

God is there for you in the dark places - and we all go through dark places. You've been knocked down, but by His grace you've always gotten up. No matter how dark the night, you've always lived to see the morning. Times change, and relationships change, but He is always the same. He's the one who brought you through the past, and He promises to be with you every day of the future. You will rise again! Motivation to survive comes from a well that you already possess within. The Lord is the one who fills that well. Let it flow. You don't have to make it flow, just let it flow.

No matter what you're going through right now, don't stop until you see the morning. It's at the end of every dark night and every broken promise, but it does come. It's at the end of setbacks, betrayals and denials, but when it's all over - morning comes. Let nothing keep you from believing that.

God will dry your tears, and you'll awake with a new song. His word says, "His compassions fail not, they are new every morning: great is thy faithfulness. The Lord is good unto them that wait for Him, to the soul that seeketh Him" (La 3:22-25). Yesterday ended last night. It's a new day, go out and enjoy it!

Purpose-Driven

Study the life of Thomas Edison. Anybody who can give the world the electric light, the microphone, storage batteries, sound films, phonographs, and a thousand other inventions, has much to teach us. Historians say he was driven by one word - purpose. Not pleasure, popularity, or even personal gain, but only purpose.

Here are some of the recorded principles by which he lived: (1) Work to obtain all the knowledge you can about what you want to achieve. (2) Fix your mind on your purpose. Persist! Seek! Use all the knowledge you can accumulate or learn from others. (3) Keep on searching no matter how many times you meet with disappointment. (4) Refuse to be influenced by the fact that someone else tried the same thing and failed. (5) Keep yourself 'sold' on the idea that a solution to the problem exists somewhere, and that you'll find it. Then he added, "The trouble with most people is, they quit before they ever start."

It's only when we've done our part that we can then call on God with confidence to do the things we can't. Nehemiah didn't conquer through brilliance, he conquered through prayer and perseverance (Neh 4:9). In spite of the criticism, in spite of threats, in spite of the pressure, he refused to fold his tent and run. That's why he rebuilt Jerusalem. God always honors the man or the woman with a spirit that never gives up.

If You Plan To Do It – Do It!

Redwood trees last for a 1,000 years, but most other things go relatively fast. For instance, a face-lift lasts only 6 to 10 years. A dollar bill lasts only a year. A painted white line in the road lasts only 4 months. A tornado lasts only a few minutes.

You say, "And what about me?" The average life span is now between 75 and 80. That sounds pretty good - if you're still young.

The Bible says your life is like a vapor, and vapors aren't known for their longevity; just a puff of smoke and they're gone! So why are you still waiting? It could be now or never; you don't have forever, so get at it!

You say you've always wanted to play the piano. Fine, start taking lessons! Or that you've always dreamed of taking a trip to the Holy Land. Call a travel agent! You say you hate your bathroom wallpaper. Scrape it off and paint it! You say you feel better when you exercise. Stop talking and start jogging! Or that you love the taste of homegrown tomatoes. Plant some! You say you're angry about the potholes in your street. Go to your town meetings! Whatever you've been putting off, do it now – tomorrow may be too late.

You think you're too old? Not a chance! The older the fiddle the sweeter the tune. Put your life into God's hands today and let Him show you what He can do with it!

No Pain, No Gain

James says, "Blessed is the man who perseveres under trial, because when he has stood the test, he will receive the crown..." (Jas 1:12 NIV).

A great illustration of this is the life of Abraham Lincoln. It reads like a biography of a failure. He had less than one year of formal schooling and failed miserably in business in 1831. He was defeated for the legislature the following year. He failed again in business a year later. His fiancé died in 1835. He was defeated for Speaker of the House in 1838. He married into what historians call "a living misery" in 1842. Only one of his four sons lived past the age of 18. He was defeated again for Congress in 1843, elected to Congress in 1846, defeated for Congress in 1848, defeated for the Senate in 1855, defeated for Vice-president in 1856, defeated for the Senate in 1858, and became one of America's greatest presidents in 1860. The road to victory is often through multiple defeats.

Without pain and problems, what real joy is there in progress? If it costs nothing, it means nothing. Learning to overcome adversity and failure is an inevitable part of achieving success. The key is perseverance. That's why David cried "My heart is fixed, oh God, my heart is fixed" (Ps 57:7). Ask God today to give you a mind that is made up and a heart that is fixed. He'll do it too!

Are You Satisfied With What You're Becoming?

In the Bay of Naples, there's a jellyfish that loves to swallow a certain snail. But the snail has a hard shell, and the jellyfish can't digest it. The snail ends up fastening itself to the inside of the jellyfish, and then slowly begins to eat it. By the time the snail is fully-grown, it has consumed the entire jellyfish. Now the point is that a lot of the things we think we can handle, like alcohol, worry, greed, or simply the aimlessness of our lives, end up consuming us.

Fred Smith, the author of "Learning to Lead," once sent all his friends a letter with these three questions: 1. Am I enjoying what I'm doing? 2. Am I happy with where I'm going? 3. Am I satisfied with what I'm becoming? One of his friends, a top Wall Street broker, called him back and said, "When I read the question, 'Am I satisfied with what I'm becoming?' I said, 'Absolutely not!' I'm tired of grabbing the Wall Street Journal first thing every morning like it's my Bible. My life has no meaning outside of my investments, so, today I liquidated them all - I'm quitting! Tomorrow I'm beginning a new life, and I want to thank you for giving me the courage to do it."

Don't end your life feeling empty, having your insides eaten away by a quest for things that can't satisfy. God has a wonderful plan for your life (Jer 29:11). Get into His presence today and let Him tell you about it.

Staying Power

Austin O'Malley says, "The fact that you have been knocked down is interesting, but the length of time you stay down is all that's really important." You need to reconcile yourself to the fact that as you travel through life, you'll have problems and you'll stumble. The question is, "Are you going to stay down or are you going to get back up and keep going?" Are you going to be like the man who said, "I'm never down; I'm either up - or getting up!" A lot of folks don't think that way. They've been down so long that they're comfortable there - and they'll even trip you up just to have company. Look out for them!

Here are some scriptures that will give you the staying power to reach your goal.

1. "For in the day of trouble He will keep me safe...He will hide me in the shelter of His tabernacle and set me high upon a rock...I am still confident of this: I will see the goodness of the Lord in the land of the living" (Ps 27:5 & 13 NIV).

2. "Blessed is the man who perseveres under trial, because when he has stood the test, he will receive the crown of life that God has promised to those who love Him" (Jas 1:12 NIV).

3. "My flesh and my heart may fail, but God is the strength of my heart and my portion forever" (Ps 73:26 NIV).

4. "Do not throw away your confidence; it will be richly rewarded. You need to persevere so that when you have done the will of God, you will receive what He has promised" (Heb 10:35-36 NIV).

These promises are yours; claim them today!

Pray for Grace

Stop worrying about whether God's going to accept you when you pray! There's nothing you can do to make Him love you more than He already does, and nothing you can do to make Him love you less. Just speak from your heart, be real and stop looking at the clock. You're not being graded on a test or running a marathon - you're talking to your Father.

The Lord's prayer consists of only 56 words. Compare that with 26,911 words in the U.S. government order setting the official price of cabbage. God deliver us from bureaucracy in government and in prayer. We are to "come boldly to the throne of our gracious God. There we will receive His mercy, and we will find grace to help us when we need it" (Heb 4:5 NLT).

What is this "grace" that we get when we pray? Gerald Brooks says, "Grace is the strength to stand and take it, it's the will to hold on to a job that stinks, a marriage that gets difficult, or a promise I could break. It's the power to let go of what others are holding on to - my achievements, my social class, my possessions, my power. It's the strength to grasp what lasts and the will to let go of what vanishes. None of that is possible on our own, it's simply a gift from God, and we get it through prayer." In other words, grace will not give you the easy way out, but it will show you the right way through - and you'll be stronger on the other side of it!

Down, But Not Out

Nothing changed for the prodigal son until he decided to get up, start moving in the right direction and accept responsibility for his life. God will go to great lengths to help you, but He can do nothing for you if you just lie there! If you accept your failure as final, then you're finally a failure - but not until then. The prodigal son discovered that his future was just waiting for him to make a decision. So is yours!

John Maxwell says, "Failing doesn't mean I'm a failure; it just means I have not yet succeeded. It doesn't mean I've accomplished nothing; it just means I've learned something. It doesn't mean I've been a fool; it just means I've had the courage to take a risk. It doesn't mean I'm inferior; it just means I'm not perfect. It doesn't mean I've wasted my time; it just means I have a reason to start over. It doesn't mean I should give up; it just means I have to try harder. It doesn't mean I'll never make it; it just means I need more patience. It doesn't mean God has abandoned me; it just means He has a better idea!"

Be encouraged today, child of God. Your Father wants to redeem you from your failures, to release you from the trap you're in and to restore you to fellowship with Him. He's waiting for you to turn to Him today with all your heart.

Keep Pressing On

Most successful people were usually just "hungrier and thirstier." What we desired, they pursued. Napoleon was born in poverty. In school his friends made fun of him, but he devoted himself to his books and excelled in his studies, and eventually he became the brightest student in the whole school. Before he was through, he conquered the world.

If a seedling tree has to fight its way up through stones and hard soil to get to sunlight and air, and then wrestle with the storm and the frost to survive, you can be sure of one thing - its root system will be strong, and it's timber will be valuable.

It is impossible to succeed without going through adversity. If you're successful and haven't experienced it, you can be sure that someone else has experienced it for you. If you're experiencing it without succeeding, there's a good chance somebody else will succeed one day because of you. Either way, there's no success without endurance.

The true test of your character is seeing what it takes to stop you! Dr. G. Campbell Morgan tells of a man whose shop had been burned in the great Chicago fire. He arrived at the ruins the next morning carrying a table. He set it up amidst the charred debris, and put a big sign above it that read, "Everything lost except wife, children and hope - business will resume as usual tomorrow morning!"

Ponder that statement for a moment!

Going Beyond the Barriers

At a coastal aquarium in Florida, a big barracuda tried to attack a mackerel, but a glass barrier that separated them prevented it. After bumping his nose into it repeatedly, he finally quit trying. Later, when the barrier was removed, the barracuda would swim to the point where the barrier had been - but no further. To him, that barrier was still there. Are you like that? Do you have imaginary barriers in your mind that say, "So far and no further?"

When God called Jeremiah, the first things out of Jeremiah's mouth were excuses about being too young, being unqualified, and not being able to do the job. Immediately God said, "Don't say that..." (Jer 1:7 NLT). There are certain things you've got to stop saying if you're ever going to break through your mental barriers and self-imposed limitations. What God said to Jeremiah, He's also saying to you: "You will go where I send you, and you'll do what I enable you to do, and whatever I have promised will come to pass in your life" (Jer 1:7 paraphrased).

God wants to change your conditioned response patterns and false belief systems. Instead of seeing what you expect, He wants you to see what's possible. Instead of thinking the worst, He wants you to look for the best, because that is what He has in mind for you today.

Keep Fighting

In the 14th Century the Emperor Tamerlane (descendant of Genghis Kahn) was badly defeated in battle. As he lay hidden in a barn, enemy troops scoured the countryside looking for him. Suddenly he noticed an ant trying to push a kernel of corn that was bigger than him, up over a wall. Sixty-nine times the ant failed, but on the seventieth try he succeeded. Leaping to his feet, Tamerlane shouted, "If you can do it, I can too." He reorganized his forces, went back, and soundly defeated the enemy.

If you're under attack today, listen to the words of Joab, "Be strong and let us fight bravely for... the Lord will do what is good..." (2Sa 10:12 NIV). Joab knew that if you do your part, God will do the rest. Child of God, keep fighting! As long as you're on the battlefield, God can give you victory!

And keep these 7 things clearly in mind:

1. Never give up if you know you're right.

2. Believe that all things work together for good, if you just persevere.

3. Don't let the odds discourage you - God's bigger than all of them.

4. Never let anyone intimidate you or deter you from your goals.

5. Fight and overcome every limitation.

6. Remember, every winner has dealt with defeat and adversity.

7. Try again, and again, and yet again, for in God's strength you'll surely succeed.

Chapter Five

A Sense of Compassion

Do You Care?

Nobody knew who he was. Nobody even seemed to care. They found him lying in a heap, with a deep gash in his throat. A doctor used black sewing thread to suture the wound, and then he was dumped into a paddy wagon and dropped off at Bellevue Hospital. There he languished until he died.

A friend seeking him went to the local morgue, and there among dozens of nameless corpses, he found him. His only possessions were a ragged coat that smelled of liquor, with 38 cents in one pocket and a scrap of paper in the other. On it was written, "Dear friends and gentle hearts." It almost sounded like the words of a song somebody was going to write.

Which would have been correct – for once upon a time this man had written songs that made the whole world sing. Songs like – "Jeannie With the Light Brown Hair," "My Old Kentucky Home," "Oh! Suzanna," and 200 more that are deeply rooted in our heritage. His name was Stephen Collins Foster.

So many people around you today are hurting. Some of them are hard to spot because they wear the mask of success. Others are clearly down and out.

How do you change the world around you? One life at a time! But you've got to care. Care enough to love, to restore, and to rekindle the flame that life has snuffed out. Consider it carefully, and then go out today and touch one person – just one - with God's love!

Dreams That Always Come True

If Solomon is correct, all you need is one dream to come true to get you moving forward. Here are three that always come true.

1. If your dream is to become rich by giving, it'll always come true. But if your dream is to become rich by getting, you'll never get enough - or if you do, you'll become poor protecting it. When you give, you're declaring that you have enough to let some go, which means you're rich! On the other hand, if you're too poor to be generous, you'll always be poor because you'll never have enough.

2. If your dream is to become happy by helping others, it'll always come true. When you help others, you're using your power. If you have the power to help, it means you're not helpless, because helping makes you focus on your strengths, not your weaknesses. On the other hand, if your dream is to become happy by using others, you'll never be happy - for others can't make you happy and you'll only "use up" every relationship you've got, and keep having to find others.

3. If your dream is to become fearless by trusting God, it'll always come true. There's only one way to become fearless - trust in something that you know will never let you down! David found it and proclaimed, "The Lord is my light and my salvation - whom shall I fear? The Lord is the stronghold of my life - of whom shall I be afraid? (Ps 27:1-2 NIV). What assurance! You'll never find anything more dependable than God!

Try To Be More Understanding

The ability to understand others is a choice, and you have to make that choice every day. Here are two tips to help you:

First, try to see it their way! Author Mark McCormick tells of standing in a ticket line where two children were fighting over an ice-cream cone. In front of them was a woman in an expensive mink coat; this was an accident just waiting to happen. As he wondered whether he should interfere, suddenly one child said to the other, "If you don't stop, you'll get hairs from that lady's coat on your ice-cream cone." When you're self-centered, your ice-cream cone will always be more important than somebody else's fur coat. But you can change. As sure as the law of gravity is defeated every time a jet leaves the ground, so the law of selfishness is conquered every time you decide to care for others, even at the expense of yourself (Ro 8:2).

Second, have a positive attitude toward people. The Bible says, "Love... always looks for the best..." (1 Co 13:7 TM). You'll generally see what you're looking for, whether it's the best or the worst. Someone once said, "When the other fellow takes a long time, he's slow. When I do, I'm thorough. When he does something without being told, he's overstepping. When I do, it's initiative. When he overlooks the rules, he's rude. When I do, I'm just being original. When he pleases his boss, he's 'an apple polisher.' When I do, I'm just being dedicated. When he gets ahead, he's lucky. When I do, it's well earned!"

Today, think of everybody you meet as the most important person in the world, because in God's eyes - they are!

Influencing Others

You can't make the other fellow feel important in your presence if you secretly feel like he's a nobody. When Jesus said, "Love one another," He was using a Greek word which means "to nurture." If you want to know what that means, think of a mother and her child. Her love for him is constant, and her greatest desire for him is that he should thrive. You may be saying to yourself, "But isn't that something they should get somewhere else, like at home?" The truth is, many of the people you know are in desperate need of being nurtured, and they'll be influenced most by those who make them feel best about themselves. If you want to influence their lives, become a nurturer.

And check your motives carefully. Don't be like the little girl who announced one Sunday on her way home from church, "When I grow up, I want to be like the man who stood up in the pulpit today." Her mom said, "You want to be a minister?" she said, "No, I just want to tell people what to do!" You may smile, but a lot of us just want to become authority figures to correct people, reveal their weak areas, and give them so-called constructive advice. John Knox said: "You can't antagonize and influence at the same time." He's right.

That's why Jesus said, "My command is this: love each other as I have loved you" (Jn 15:12 NIV). That kind of love seeks only the best, and believes only the best. If you find yourself needing more of it, get into God's presence today and ask Him for it, because it is "the fruit of the spirit..."(Gal 5:22NIV).

Are You Compassionate?

Every time you see people with unnatural fear in their eyes, low self-esteem, or an apologetic posture, they're silently crying, "Don't you care that I perish?" (Mk 4:38 paraphrased). We can build churches on every corner, and decorate them with the finest tapestries and artifacts, but if people can't find compassion and solutions among us, they'll pass through unchanged by our programs, our politics, or our pronouncements.

Do you have a compassionate attitude? Or are you like the pastor who returned from a preaching trip and was met by one of his members at the train station. The man said, "Pastor, a tornado wiped out our home." The pastor replied, "I'm not surprised, given the way you've been living!" The man continued, "It also destroyed your house too, Pastor." Stunned into silence, the good reverend finally said, "Ah, the ways of the Lord are past human understanding!"

Don't wait until calamity touches you before you have compassion for others. Reach out with a strong hand and a soft heart, and touch them with the love of God. Listen carefully to these words: "clothe yourselves with tender-hearted mercy... make allowance for each other's faults... the most important piece of clothing you must wear is love..." (Col 3:12-14 NLT). Now there's something to think about!

Put Yourself In Their Place

Voltaire tells of a king whose favorite horse was lost, so he offered a great reward. Many wise men tried to find it and failed; but a simpleton in his court found it and brought it back. "How did you do it?" asked the king. The man simply replied, "I thought, if I were a horse, where would I go? Putting myself in his place, I soon found him!"

Compassion is simply putting yourself in somebody else's place. It's asking God to help you understand and discern what is really going on with them. It's hearing what they're not saying, as well as what they are saying, so that you understand their anger is only masking their fear, and they're crying out for help in the only way they know how.

Before Peter failed and denied the Lord, Jesus said to him, "...When thou art converted, strengthen thy brethren" (Lk 22:32). When grace touches your life, you'll always reach back for others!

Quit acting like you made it on your own. It was only God's grace that brought you through, right? Go ahead and reach out to others in love. If they reject you, they'll only push you closer to the crucified life. But if they accept you, tell them, "Whatever you need, God has it. In spite of your circumstances it can be done!" The heart of the Gospel is that God loved us enough to come to where we were, so that we would love others enough to go to where they are.

Loving Others

Think about the people who have influenced your life most. Weren't they the people who cared about you most and took the time to show it? John Maxwell tells of a teacher who made a difference in the life of a student. The teacher wrote: "I had a great feeling of relief when I began to understand that a youngster needs more than just subject matter. I know mathematics well and I teach it well, and I used to think that was all I needed to do. Now I teach children, not math. I also know now that I can only succeed with some of them, and that I don't have to 'have all the answers.' The funny thing is, I seem to have more answers when I stop trying to be the expert. The youngster who really made me understand this was Eddie. One day I asked him why he thought he was doing so much better this year than last year. I'll never forget his answer; 'Because when I'm with you, I like myself better!'"

Eddie responded to love in a way that he would never have responded to knowledge or technique. When he knew somebody really cared about him, he blossomed. Paul said the same thing when he said, "No matter what I say, what I believe, and what I do, I'm bankrupt without love. Love never gives up. Love cares more for others than for self...[and] always looks for the best..." (1 Co 13:4-8 TM). Why don't you read those words again, and ask God to make them a reality in your life today?

How Do You Treat Hurting People?

"Don't get sidetracked by people's pain or problems. After all, it's probably just the result of their sin. Get them converted and the problem will solve itself. Anyway, feeding the poor is something 'liberals' do!" Who thinks like that? I used to – but not anymore!

Why can't we be conservative and still be compassionate? Jesus wouldn't "give an inch" when it came to the truth, but watch Him around hurting people. "He was moved with compassion" (Mt 9:36).

Sadly, a lot of us are only moved with indignation, but then that's easier, isn't it? That way we don't have to... get our hands dirty... take risks... feel what it's like to hurt... or deal with the "thorny side" of an issue that has no easy answers. Look out! People don't care how much we know, until they first know how much we care!

A conversation took place many years ago between God and some very religious people in the Old Testament. The religious men said, "Why don't you see our sacrifices? Why don't you hear our prayers?" (Isa 58:3 LB). God's answer should make all of us do some real soul-searching. God answered, "Feed the hungry! Help those in trouble! Then... the Lord will guide you continually, and satisfy you with all good things, and keep you healthy too" (Isa 58:10-11 LB). What a promise!

Jesus said that we'd be judged and rewarded - according to how we treat hurting people (Mt 25:34-40; Col 3:12-14; Jas 5:11). So ask yourself today, "How do I treat them?"

Loving is Listening

Did you hear about the two psychiatrists? At the end of the day the older one looked as fresh as a daisy, but the younger one was frazzled. "How can you look so good after hearing patients all day?" the younger one asked. The older one replied, "It's easy. I never listen."

Listening can be exhausting, but it's the glue that holds relationships together. Nobody was busier than Jesus, but He took time to listen to people; He even sensed and shared their pain, and He says to us, "Love one another the way I loved you" (Jn 15:17). In other words, love them enough to listen.

Before you can be a good listener, you've got to deal with your own emotional baggage. Freud said, "A man with a toothache cannot be in love." Why? Because the toothache won't allow him to notice anything but his own pain. If you've never worked your way through your own "issues," you will inevitably filter what others say through them and either react defensively or try to force your opinions on them. Don't do it! If you've an ax to grind, their words will be drowned out by the sound of your grindstone.

Here are seven guidelines to help you become a better listener:

1. Listen for both content and feelings.
2. Listen with your eyes and your hearing will be improved.
3. Listen for their interest, not just their position.
4. Listen to what they are not saying.
5. Listen with compassion.
6. Listen for the areas where they are afraid or hurt.
7. Listen as you would like to be listened to.

Before You Criticize

Make sure the issue you're trying to correct is worth your time and attention. Ask yourself, "Does it really matter?" Have you allowed yourself to get distracted and needled by something insignificant, instead of keeping your eye on your goal? The Bible says, "Consider Him who endured such opposition..." (Heb 12:3 NIV). Check and see how Jesus handled the circumstances you are facing today.

Don't destroy the other person's self-confidence. Stay away from all-inclusive statements like "you always" or "you never." Assure them that you have confidence in them and in their ability to recover and handle things better next time. Correction will do much, but encouragement will do a lot more! Deal with them on an individual basis, for that's what God does. Comparisons always cause resentment, and that will get you nowhere. Why make the problem bigger?

It's always easier to be critical than it is to be creative, but unless you're willing to help, you're not qualified to get involved. Straighten out the problem, not the person. When confrontation becomes a personal attack, you destroy your own credibility and end up in a "no-win situation." Your goal should be to leave them with 3 things:

1. A clear understanding of the problem,

2. The assurance of your love, and

3. Encouragement and the confidence that they can turn it around.

That's why Paul wrote, "Carry each other's burdens..." (Gal 6:2 NIV).

Remember To Be Kind

Morris Chalfant tells of an old couple celebrating their 50th wedding anniversary. When the husband was asked what the secret of their success was, as the elderly often do, he answered with a story.

He said his wife Sarah was the only girl he'd ever dated. He'd grown up in an orphanage and worked hard for everything he had, and he never had time to date until Sarah swept him off his feet. Before he knew it, she'd managed to get him to ask her to marry him. After they had said their vows, Sarah's father took the new groom aside and handed him a small gift. He said, "This gift is all you really need to have a happy marriage." Nervously the young groom fumbled with the paper and the ribbon, until he got the package unwrapped.

In the box he found a large gold watch. As he picked it up he noticed a message etched across the face of it. Every day when he looked at his watch for the next fifty years, he would not only read the time, but he would also read the secret of a successful marriage. The words on the watch read, "Say something nice to Sarah!"

Chapter Six

A Conviction That A Basic Holiness (Goodness)
Permeates Things and People

Strive For Integrity

Nothing - absolutely nothing - is more important to your future that your personal integrity. Webster defines it in one word - honesty! You can only hide your lack of integrity for so long. Eventually, like a faulty foundation in a storm, the cracks will widen, the roof will fall in, and everything you've worked to build will be lost.

And "getting away with it" can be worse than getting caught, especially if it encourages you to believe that you can keep living at two levels. "Like a partridge that hatches eggs it did not lay, is a man who gains riches by unjust means... in the end he will prove to be a fool" (Jer 17:11 NIV).

Don't think that you can do whatever you want in small things and be okay as long as you have no major lapses. It's your first lie that makes you a liar, and whether you steal one dollar or one million dollars, you're still a thief. Phillips Brooks says, "Character is made in the small moments of our lives."

Integrity always puts character over personal gain, people over things, service over power, principal over convenience, and the long view over the immediate. Every time you break a moral principle, it becomes harder, not easier, to act with integrity.

Everything you've done in the past, including the things you've neglected to do, come to a head when you're under pressure. That's why developing and maintaining integrity requires constant vigilance. John Weston says, "Live by the following rule: don't do anything you wouldn't feel comfortable reading about in tomorrow's newspaper."

Responsibility

Admiral Rickover once said, "Responsibility is a unique concept. When you share it, your portion is still not diminished. When you delegate it, it's still with you. No amount of evasion, or ignorance, or "passing the buck" can shift it. Unless someone can point a finger at you when something goes wrong, then the truth is, you never were responsible to begin with."

God's looking for people He can entrust with responsibility. Not dreamers, but doers! Not those who stay neutral, but those who get off the fence and get the job done – whatever the cost.

Sometimes the decision to do nothing is wise, but you can't make a career out of it. Freddy Fulcrum weighed everything too carefully. He would say, "On the one hand… but then on the other…." His arguments weighed out so evenly that he never did anything. When Freddy finally died, they carved a big zero on his tombstone.

If you decide to fish, fine; if you decide to cut bait, fine; but if you decide to do nothing - you're not going to have fish for dinner.

Fulfilling God's purpose for your life means making decisions, tough decisions, lonely decisions, unpleasant decisions, misunderstood decisions, and courageous decisions. It also means the end of excuses, because "For unto whomsoever much is given, of him shall much be required" (Luke 12:48).

When The Seasons Change

Change will either bless you, or run over you like a steamroller, but either way it's going to be part of your life. When you can accept that, you're unsinkable. Parents, love your children enough to let them go. Don't be afraid that you won't be valued when you're no longer needed in the same way. You'll always be needed; it's just that the areas of need will change. The days of the cocoon may have ended, but with every flap of their wings, our children pay tribute to those who nurtured them and gave them the grace to fly. Hats off to the past, coats off to the future!

Solomon says, there's a "time to every purpose under the heaven" (Ecl 3:1). Find God's purpose for the season you're in, rediscover your assets and get moving. You haven't been "laid off," you've just been promoted. Get up rejoicing, for this is a day that somebody else missed. While you were sleeping, they gasped a final sigh, and slipped into eternity. But you are still here! Enjoy it, for there'll never be another moment like this one.

No two days are the same. They weren't meant to be. Each one is an expression of a multifaceted God, too big to be defined in just one circumstance. Every day you'll see a new aspect of His wisdom and His grace. Should you find yourself stuck at any point, just look up and pray, "God, grant me the serenity to accept the things I cannot change, the courage to change the things I can, and the wisdom to know the difference."

Always Do What's Right

Do people have to wonder about your motives? Recently I saw a cartoon where some hogs were feeding and the farmer was filling their trough to the brim. Behind them a big sign read - *Premium Bacon Company*. In the cartoon one hog was saying to the others, "Have you ever wondered why the farmer is being so good to us?"

Paul defines integrity in these words: "in honor preferring one another..." (Ro 12:10). Integrity always seeks the good of others, and believes that if something is not good for both sides, it's not good for either. Do you believe like that? If you "exploit the poor or glad-hand the rich - whichever, you'll end up the poorer for it" (Pr 22:16 TM).

If you want to check the quality of your integrity, answer these questions: How transparent am I with others? How well do I treat people from whom I can gain nothing? Do I play different roles depending on whom I'm with? Do I put others ahead of my own personal agenda? Do I love people and use things, or love things and use people? Do I make difficult decisions even when it costs me personally? When I have something to say about a person, do I talk to them or do I talk about them? Am I accountable to anybody other than myself for what I say and do?

These are some of the most important questions you'll ever answer, so take your time and consider them carefully today. You may succeed momentarily because of what you know or do, but you'll only succeed permanently because of what you are.

Needed: A Sense of Value

Adam had a relationship with God before he had one with Eve. Why? Because nobody but God can tell you who you really are, and what you're worth! Until you know that, you won't know whether you are in love - or in need. You'll keep looking for somebody to love you so that you will finally start feeling good about yourself. The trouble is, when you find that person, you'll cling to them like a vine. You'll agree with all their opinions and have none of your own. You'll try to meet their every need and make yourself indispensable. You'll feel threatened if they can do anything without you. When they enjoy somebody else's company you'll panic and say, "All I need is you, how come you don't feel the same way about me?" No human relationship can sustain such a load.

Adam learned how to relate to Eve - only after he had learned to relate to God. It's in God's presence, free from the demands of others, that you begin to look yourself in the right mirror. It's here that you prepare the gift to be given. But something has changed - now you know how much the gift is worth, and you'll only give it to someone who places the same value on it. God has always wanted the best for you; He has just been waiting for you to come into agreement with Him. The truth of the matter is that as "the Spirit of the Lord works within us, we become more and more like Him and reflect His glory..." (2Co 3:18 NLT). Why don't you spend some time with Him today, and start discovering how much you're really worth?

Wisdom For Single Parents

If you're raising your children alone, teach them the following principles. As you do, they'll be reinforced in you. You'd be surprised how many teachers learn while they teach.

First, teach them to accept change. When we get stuck in the past, it's always at the expense of the future. After the initial shock is over, and the anger has dissipated, step over your depression and start making plans. Go ahead! Announce to your heart that you're going to live again. Don't get stuck in a stage that was just meant to be part of a process. This too shall pass. Let it!

Second, teach them that past failures do not prevent future successes. We're fueled by the past, but fuel only works when it's combusted into another form. Allow the pain of your past to fuel your future with wisdom and compassion. Some of the most successful people in the world have experienced failure. This year's winner was last year's runner-up. Learn from your mistakes. Seize the new day! When you do that, anything is possible.

Third, teach them to love imperfect people. Love is a risk, but it's worth it. Hearing you say that will help your child not to become cynical. Explain to them that when we love people, we must love what's excellent, and accept what's still "under construction." It will save them from heartache if you teach them that all of us will disappoint each other, and that God's remedy for this is: "love covers over a multitude of sins" (1 Pe 4:8).

The Refiner's Fire

It takes fire to purify gold, and when God gets ready to refine us, He uses fiery trials! Nothing brings luster to your character, and commitment to your heart, like opposition. Whenever you see someone whose life reflects the character of Christ, you're looking at someone who has been through the fire.

The good news is, you may be in the fire today, but God has His hand on the thermostat! He knows the heat required to burn away the impurities that would hinder His purposes in your life. His hand fans the flames needed to teach you patience, prayer, forgiveness, faith, and a lot of other character-building lessons. You need His correction - you don't enjoy it - but you need it. After all, "All discipline for the moment seems not to be joyful, but sorrowful; yet to those who have been trained by it, afterwards it yields the peaceable fruit of righteousness" (Heb 12:11 NAS).

No one invests without expecting a return, and God is a wise businessman. He'll do whatever it takes to protect His investment in you. We spend so much of our time talking about what we want from God, when the real issue is what He wants from us - and what He'll do to get it. John said, "He'll place everything true in it's proper place... everything false He'll put out with the trash to be burned" (Mt 3:12 TM). Maybe this will help you to understand some of the things that are happening in your life at the moment.

Rejoice In Who You Are

Avoid relationships with people who don't value themselves, for they're incapable of valuing you either. Look for those who enhance you - not inhibit you - because they will fertilize your mind and put wind beneath your wings. When you're around people like that, you'll see your best qualities through their eyes, and you'll grow from the wisdom that falls from their lips.

When you encounter someone who tries to tell you that you've nothing to offer, be sure to laugh. It's impolite to hear a joke and not laugh. When God made you He said, "It was very good" (Gen 1:31). So don't give any contrary opinions the time of day. You're full of such potential that the word possibility is written all over you. By God's grace you can be anything He desires you to be.

If you're regretting your past, remember, God's looking at your future. His love for you isn't based on your performance or your virtues. Listen, "But God commendeth his love toward us, in that, while we were yet sinners, Christ died for us" (Ro 5:8). He's a God of second chances, and new horizons. Paul wrote, "There has never been the slightest doubt in my mind that the God who started this great work in you would keep at it and bring it to a flourishing finish" (Php 1:6 TM). Rejoice, because He has brought you this far and He'll take you the rest of the way. That's a promise!

Stand In Faith Believing

If you are in a fiery trial today, be advised - it's your faith that's on trial! Faith is such a key issue in Christian living that the people in the early church were actually called "believers " because of their great faith. Here are a few important things you need to know about faith, if you're going to use yours effectively.

First, faith cannot alter purpose; it's only God's agent in fulfilling it! If God's plan requires that you face opposition to accomplish His will (and it usually does), then your faith is what enables you to endure. It's like the night watchman who protects God's purpose in your life.

Second, understand that it's wonderful when God prospers you, but don't make finances the barometer of your faith! In Hebrews 11 there were two groups of faithful people; one group demonstrated such faith that their very shadow healed the sick, and other group's faith enabled them to bleed to death beneath a pile of stones for the cause of Christ (Heb 11:37). It is important to note: both groups "obtained a good report through faith " (Heb 11:39).

Shadrach, Meshach, and Abednego discovered that when God is with you in the fire, three things always happen: 1. The thing the enemy hopes will destroy you will actually reposition you and set you free. 2. The heat that destroys others won't affect you because He's there with you. 3. When you come out of the fire, you'll have a testimony that will convince both friends and foes alike.

You Can Change Your Life If You Want To

Here are some steps you can take today

1   Discern what success really is! When others feel good about you, you're popular, but when you feel good about yourself, you're successful. Your life's highest calling is usually whatever creates the highest level of joy within you. That doesn't mean it will either be easy or pain-free. Every winner in history paid a price, and so will you!

2   Prayerfully set goals. Success is achieving the goals God has for you. It's not wrong to set goals, it's just wrong to worry about the future. Solomon said, "We should make plans - counting on God to direct us" (Pr 16:9 TLB). What are your goals? How do you plan to reach them?

3   Stop looking for somebody else to bring you happiness! Don't wait for flowers to arrive; God gave you seed, start growing your own. We are to "Let every man prove his own work... then he shall have rejoicing in himself alone, and not in another" (Gal 6:4). When you're less "needy," you'll be more attractive.

4   Get over yourself – everyone one else has! A friend of mine says he was praying one day, "Father, why does the enemy keep reminding me of the same things over and over?" and God replied, "Because he's running low on material!" What a great answer! God says He will not remember your sins (Isa 43:25). So unless you're better than Him - do the same thing!

Now make these four principles part of your life

How Well Do You Handle Criticism?

If you ever do anything worthwhile, you'll take some flak! Jesus did, and He said, "The servant is not greater than his Lord" (Jn 15:20). Remember that next time somebody shoots at you.

Take a moment and consider these words by Theodore Roosevelt: "It's not the critic who counts nor the man who points out where the strong man stumbled or how the doer of deeds could have done better. No! The credit belongs to the man who is actually in the arena; whose face is marred by dust and sweat and blood. Who strives valiantly; who errs and comes up short again and again, because there is no effort without error or shortcoming; who spends himself in a worthy cause; who, at worst, if he fails, at least fails while daring greatly. Far better is it to dare mighty things than to rank with those poor souls who neither enjoy nor suffer, because they live in the gray twilight that knows neither victory nor defeat."

Perhaps you need to read that again – especially if you've been criticized lately. Ultimately it's not what others say about you that matters; what really counts is what you say to yourself - after they get through talking.

Building Character

Did you hear about the Wall Street broker who fell in love with a rising Broadway actress? Before proposing marriage, he decided to have a private investigator check her out. "After all," he thought, "I've got a lot to lose." He asked the agency not to reveal his identity to the investigator making the report. When it came back, the report said, "She has an excellent character, an unblemished past, and a great future. But we have one concern: she's been seen lately with a young Wall Street Broker whose reputation is very questionable." You may smile, but the Bible says the truth spoke well of a man named Demetrius. The question is, what does the truth say about you?

Reputation is perception, but character is reality! It's what you are in the dark. It's a commitment you make to yourself before the hour of testing comes. It's having values you refuse to violate either for profit or advantage. It's a wall of integrity built brick by brick and day by day, and it's hard work!

Until you can learn to trust yourself, your goals will have to wait. God will allow you to pass through situations that bring to the surface areas that must be dealt with. And you'll stay there until you deal with them. Why don't you get alone with God today and pray, "Search me, Oh God, and know my heart..." (Ps 139:23 NIV). Then listen to what He has to say to you.

Chapter Seven

We Find Ourselves In Loyal Commitments

Maturity

Maturity is the ability to control your anger, and settle your differences without violence or resentment. Read that again, carefully.

Maturity is patience; it's the willingness to pass up immediate pleasure for long-term gain. It's the ability to "sweat it out" in spite of heavy opposition or discouraging setbacks. It's the capacity to face unpleasantness and frustration without complaining or collapsing.

Maturity is humility. It's being big enough to say, "I was wrong," and when you're right, never needing to say "I told you so."

Maturity is the ability to make a decision and follow through on it, instead of exploring endless possibilities and doing nothing about any of them.

Maturity means dependability, keeping your word and coming through in a crisis. The immature are masters of alibi; they are confused and disorganized. Their lives are a maze of broken promises, former friends, unfinished business, and good intentions.

Maturity is the art of being at peace with what you can't change, having the courage to change what you can, and the wisdom to know the difference. Are you maturing?

Get In Or Get Out

Walter Haley, one of the world's greatest insurance salesmen, had a rocky start. Doors closed, quotas were not met, discouragement set in, and he wondered, "Am I going to make it?"

One day he told his boss, "I'm quitting!" The boss said, "You can't." Walter said, "Oh yes I can." Again the boss said, "You can't." Finally, Walter got hot under the collar and said, "Well, I am quitting." At that moment the boss said something that changed the rest of Walter Haley's life. He said, "Son, you can't get out of the insurance business, because you never really got into it."

Whatever you're doing today, if you can't get into it, get out of it and find something you can give your best to. The key to will power is want power. You have to want it enough to get up earlier, stay up later, and do whatever it takes. Failures want what successes have, but they just don't want to pay what successes paid to get it.

When Albert Schweitzer was 30, he decided to study medicine and go to Africa as a missionary. Everybody thought he'd lost his mind. He was already a renowned musician, philosopher, and theologian. Why would you enter medical school as a freshman, then bury yourself in a jungle? Listen to his reply, "I can do it - and I must do it!" Today look deep within and ask yourself, "What is it that I can do, and that I must do?" When you find the answer - you'll find your destiny.

Gossip – Remember Me?

Consider these words carefully: "I maim without killing. I break hearts and ruin lives. I am cunning and malicious, and I gather strength with age. The more I am quoted, the more I am believed. I flourish at every level of society. My victims are helpless; they cannot protect themselves against me because I have no name and no face. To track me down is impossible. The harder you try, the more illusive I become. I am nobody's friend. Once I tarnish a reputation it's never the same. I topple governments. I wreck marriages. I make innocent people cry. Who am I? My name is gossip!"

Jesus said, "Every idle word that men shall speak, they shall give account thereof in the day of judgement. For by thy words thou shalt be justified, and by thy words thou shalt be condemned" (Mt 12:36-37).

Do you really believe that? If you do, you won't break someone's heart by spreading their secrets, betraying their confidence, ruining their good name, or undermining their self-esteem with ridicule and innuendoes. You just won't do it!

David prayed, "Take control of what I say O Lord, and keep my lips sealed" (Ps 141:3 NLT). That would be a good prayer for you to pray today too!

Lifting Others

The first black-American to play major-league baseball was Jackie Robinson. He faced terrible insults and abuse in every stadium, while trying to break through baseball's color barrier. One day in his home stadium in Brooklyn, he committed 'an error,' and immediately the fans turned on him. While they jeered, he just stood there at second base, humiliated.

At that point, shortstop Pee Wee Reese ran over, stood next to him, put his arm around him, and together they faced the crowd. Within seconds the fans grew quiet. Years later, when Robinson was elected to Baseball's Hall of Fame, he said, "It was Reese's arm around my shoulder that day that saved my career."

When Jesus lifted and restored Peter after his shameful denial, He told him, "strengthen thy brethren" (Lk 22:32). If God lifts you, you'll want to lift others! It'll be as natural to you as breathing.

That is what true friends do. Jonathan, Saul's son, "arose and went to David in the woods and strengthened his hand in God." (1Sa 23:16). In prosperity our friends know us, but in adversity we know our friends; they're the ones who come to us when we're "in the woods." Are you a friend like that? If you think you'll ever need one - be one.

Four Things You Should Give Your Children

First, listen to them! One boy said, "I'm just a comma. When I talk to my Dad, he'll say something. Then when I start to talk, he makes a comma; he doesn't interrupt me, but when I'm finished talking, he starts right in where he left off. It's as if I didn't say anything." You'll never understand your child until you really listen to what he or she is saying.

Second, believe in them. As a child, the great Caruso was told by a music teacher, "You have no talent at all." Parent, make sure your voice is the loudest. Get there first; build their confidence; make them a "can-do" person; give them faith to overcome every obstacle in life.

Third, connect with them! Find out what's in their heart. If you try to control them before you connect with them, you'll lose them. What do you really know about them? Their music? Their heroes? Their friends? Their concerns? If your answer is, "Not much," then start making some changes right now.

Fourth, let them see God in you! Have you heard the story of three kids discussing their dads? One said, "My Dad knows the mayor." Another said, "My Dad knows the governor." Confidently, the third said, "That's nothing - my Dad knows God!" Parent, do you know God? If you don't, commit your life to Him today.

Pour Yourself Into Someone Else

The greatest investment you can make - is in people! That's what God did; He invested His son into humanity, and empowered us to go out and demonstrate how His Kingdom works.

If you've achieved any level of success, pour it into somebody else. If you've outgrown your need for a father or mother, be one to some desperate young man or woman whose natural ties are broken. Plant in them the things you want to say to the next generation.

In 1924, the English artist William Wolcott visited the office of a friend in New York. Seeing a piece of paper on his desk, Wolcott asked, "May I have that?" His friend answered, "But it's not sketching paper, it's just wrapping paper." Not wanting to lose his inspiration, Wolcott took the wrapping paper and replied, "Nothing is ordinary, if you know how to use it."

On that ordinary paper he made two simple sketches. Later that year one of them sold for $500 and the other for $1,000, a princely sum in 1924. People under the influence of an empowering person are like paper in the hands of a great artist - no matter what they're made of, they can become treasures.

Let Him Prove It - At The Altar

When a man tells you to "prove your love" by committing fornication with him, tell him to read this: "Girls need to prove their love through illicit sex, like a moose needs a hat-rack."

Why not prove your love by sticking your head in the oven, and turning on the gas! Or how about playing leapfrog in the traffic? It's about as safe. Clear the cobwebs out of your head! Anybody who asks you to prove your love is trying to take you for the biggest, most gullible fool that ever walked. That "proving" bit is one of the rottenest lines ever invented.

Does he love you? It doesn't sound like it. Someone who loves you wants whatever is best for you. Figure it out; he wants you to commit an immoral act, surrender your virtue, throw away your self-respect, risk the loss of your reputation, and risk getting pregnant, getting diseased, and getting into trouble. That's the biggest laugh of the century!

He wants what's best for him! He wants a thrill he can brag about at your expense. Love? Who's kidding whom? A guy who loves a girl would sooner cut off his right arm than hurt her. In my opinion, this self-serving individual has proved that he doesn't love you at all.

The predicable aftermath always finds Don Juan tiring of his sport. That's when he drops you, picks up his line, and goes casting elsewhere for another equally foolish fish. If he loves you, let him prove his love - at the altar.

So You Want To Be A Leader

Jerusalem lay in ruins. That's where Nehemiah enters the picture (Neh 6). He rallied, motivated, and organized the people. Fifty-two days later, they washed off their trowels, stowed their gear, and walked away from a newly finished wall. How did he do it?

1   He had passion! He could hardly sleep at night for picturing the problem and seeing himself solving it. That's what it takes!

2   He could motivate others! What good is your leadership if you can't move other people to action?

3   He had confidence in God! He may have doubted his own ability, but he never doubted God's. His book is full of prayers — silent ones, short ones, and specific ones.

4   He refused to give up! From the moment he started mixing the mortar until the day he hung the last gate, his critics never "let up." But he took it — sarcasm, suspicion, gossip, threats, false accusations — you name it. Nothing could move him.

5   He was realistic! He had some of the workers building the wall while others stood guard against attack. He acted without over-reacting; he was gracious but unbending. Good leaders may have their head in the heavens, but they've got their feet on the ground.

6   He had the discipline to finish the job. Good leaders are finishers. When the job loses its luster, they don't go somewhere else; they stay at it "in season and out."

Do you still want to be a leader?

Please – Remember The Forgotten

The religion that God our Father accepts is this: "to look after orphans and widows…" (Jas 1:27 NIV). This could be the opportunity you've been looking for! The only qualification you need is the memory of how it feels to be "left out" and the compassion to do something about it.

A woman whose husband died wrote a letter she called, "The Story of Widowhood." The letter reads: "First numbness, then busyness. A million things to settle. Endless death certificates and things to sign. Friends are so considerate; caring support from relatives. You keep busy.

"But at night you pound the empty side of the bed in grief. Finally you close your eyes, throw his toothbrush into the garbage, and toss out the old work shoes you brought home from the hospital in a plastic bag. You empty the closet and give all his things away. It's a heartache like you wouldn't believe. Every suit reminds you of a special place or time you shared together.

"A year has passed; you're still in one piece. Then the blow! Your friends celebrate a birthday - all couples. You're not included because you'd be a 'fifth wheel.' Some wives even consider you a threat.

"Please remember us. Don't treat us like excess baggage. We've been handed a rotten break, and we need friends."

Then she signed it – Forgotten.

Think of the difference you could make today in somebody's life if you were just willing to "remember the forgotten."

Learning To Live Together

Take away one link and the chain breaks. Take away one player and the game is lost. Even a tiny screw, if it falls out of your carburetor, can bring the whole car to a screeching halt. What's the point? Simply this – we need each other! John Donne wrote, "No man is an island," so let's stop acting like one.

To make life work you have to learn how to - lean on others, yet know how to lend them your support; be generous enough to give, yet always be humble enough to receive; be honest enough to confess, yet always be willing to forgive. Are you getting the idea?

Love and acceptance are not optional... neither is tolerance... or understanding... or patience. You know - all those things you need from others when your "humanity" crowds out your "divinity."

The Word says, "Take delight in honoring each other. Be patient in trouble, and prayerful always. When God's children are in need, you be the one to help them out" (Ro 12:10-13 LB).

You say, "Why should I do that?" Because each of us is worth it, even when we don't act like it or feel like it or deserve it. Furthermore, since none of us is a whole, independent, self-sufficient, super-capable, all-powerful hotshot, let's quit acting like we are. Life's lonely enough without playing that game!

Real Relationships

The purpose of God in your life is tied to certain relationships. They're the ones who stand by you. Remember Jonathan who loved David, even at the cost of his own life? Or Ruth who loved Naomi and gave her a reason to live again? God has people like that, and you need them. He wouldn't say, "It's not good that man should be alone," (Gen 2:18) and then make you live in isolation.

But you need to be healed before you can enter new relationships and make healthy choices. You need to learn to differentiate between 'using' relationships and 'heart-ties.' Blood-ties don't wear as well as heart-ties.

Allow God to work on you. When you're ready, He'll make all the necessary introductions. In the meantime, get to know Him better. Make His opinion the source of your self worth. If your last relationship stripped you of your identity and drained you spiritually, then use this precious time to get back on your feet. You may never have this opportunity again!

Begin today to love like God loves. He sees your imperfection, handles your rejection - and loves you regardless. That should help you not to throw away a good person, simply because they happened to fail you. Would you discard your car over a leaky radiator? If God forgave you as you forgive others, could you stand? (Ps 130:3). Today, ask God to teach you about real relationships.

Chapter Eight

Not Needing To Force Our Way

Recognizing Others

In a recent survey, the number one cause of discontent amongst workers was - failure on the part of their superiors to share recognition and show appreciation! It's hard to follow somebody, no matter how great their vision may be, if they never take time to appreciate you for who you are, and for what you do.

Former Secretary of State, Robert McNamara, says, "Brains are like hearts; they usually go where they're appreciated!" Virginia Arcastle adds, "When people are made to feel important, it's no longer necessary for them to whittle down others, in order to seem bigger by comparison." Consider that! In Romans 16, Paul takes an entire chapter to recognize those who had helped him, including Phoebe who was "...worthy of high honor."

If you're one of those high-energy, self-starter types who thinks you don't need encouragement (and therefore why would anybody else?), ponder these words by William Ward: "Flatter me, and I may not believe you. Criticize me, and I may not like you. Ignore me, and I may not forgive you. But encourage me, and I'll never forget you!"

Have you any idea how many people around you today, including some highly placed ones, are battling defeat, despair, depression, and a sense of worthlessness? Go and speak to them; give them the encouragement they need – because they need it.

The Art of Gentleness

Mr. Myrick had to go to Chicago on business, and he persuaded his brother to take care of his cat while he was gone. Myrick's brother was not a cat lover, but he agreed to do it anyway. When Myrick returned, he called his brother from the airport, and asked, "How's the cat?" His brother said in a cold matter-of-fact voice, "Your cat's dead!"

For days Myrick was inconsolable. Then his grief turned to anger, and he called his brother back and said, "It was cruel of you to do that."

"What did you expect me to do?" demanded his brother.

"You could have broken the news gradually," said Myrick. "First, you could say the cat was playing on the roof. Next you could say he fell off. The next morning you could say he had broken his leg. Then when I came to pick him up, you could say he passed away peacefully in the night. But being gentle was never your style! Now tell me, how's mama?" After a long pause, a meek voice on the other end of the phone replied, "She's playing on the roof."

Myrick's insensitive brother had finally learned the art of gentleness.

Gentleness is a mixture of patience, sensitivity, and concern for the feelings of others. It's a product of the spirit, not the flesh. It's literally allowing God to work through you to bring healing and solutions. Ask Him today to give it to you!

Living is Giving

If you want to be like Jesus, forget about yourself and live for others, for that's what He did! Mark 10:45 says, "For even the Son of man did not come to be served, but to serve, and to give His life as a ransom for many." Don't pray for a generous heart; practice being generous and your heart will follow. Become a sower and God will give you more seed (2 Co 9:10). If He's not giving you all the seed you want, it could be that you haven't become a sower yet.

And always do more than you're expected to do. Rebecca did that, and she became the bride of Isaac and the inheritor of all Abraham's blessings (Gen 24). Have you any idea how much water one thirsty camel can drink? Well, Rebecca watered a whole train of them for a perfect stranger, and even though she didn't know it, she was writing the resume for her future. Don't pass up an opportunity to give or to be gracious, for you have no idea whose camels you're watering.

Instead of always having to be the bride at the wedding and the corpse at the funeral, learn to put others first. Follow the example of the Macedonians who "gave not only what they could afford, but far more... their first action was to dedicate themselves to the Lord and to us, for whatever directions God might give them through us" (2 Co 8:3-5 LB). Now there's a formula for making your life count!

Let God Promote You

If you don't find your significance and your self-worth in God, you'll spend your life trying to promote yourself. That will make you both insecure and dangerous. Why? Because when others are promoted ahead of you, you'll become resentful, and you may even try to tear them down. In God's Kingdom you don't achieve spiritual success - you receive it from God, because "God is the judge; He putteth down one, and setteth up another" (Ps 75:5-7).

While David's brothers were striving to be king and "get the nod" from the prophet Samuel, David just kept tending his sheep and doing what God had told him to do. Let others strive for crowns and thrones; just be faithful to what God has given you - and when you're ready, He'll come and get you. That's a promise!

Jesus said, "...My yoke is easy, and my burden is light" (Mt 11:30). Did you hear that? When He gives something to you, it'll come easy. That doesn't mean it won't require hard work. It just means you won't have to strive to get it, or strive to keep it. And only He can take it away, and He doesn't do that unless like Saul, you become rebellious, unfaithful, and refuse to repent. Knowing all that takes all the strain out of serving Him, doesn't it?

Ducks and Rabbits

Every creature God makes has a unique set of abilities capable of making it excel. On the land a duck waddles, but in the water it glides. A rabbit runs with ease, but have you ever seen one swimming laps? Eagles are great in the air, but lousy in a foot race; there the rabbit will beat the eagle every time – unless of course the eagle is hungry.

Whether you're a creature in the forest or a Christian in the family, God made you with special gifts. There are no big gifts and little gifts. We say stuff like that, but God doesn't!

1 Corinthians 12 is dedicated to getting each of us to identify our gifts, and then to develop them to the max. It teaches you that when you operate according to your gift, you excel and the whole body benefits - and you experience incredible satisfaction.

But when you compare, force, or entertain expectations beyond your reach, you just get frustrated, discouraged, and before long, you give up in defeat.

So if God made you a "duck" saint – swim like mad and don't get bent out of shape because you waddle when you run. Furthermore, if you're an "eagle" saint, stop expecting squirrels to soar or rabbits to build the same kind of nest you do. Accept your spiritual gift, cultivate it, stop comparing it to somebody else's, and start enjoying what God's called you to be!

Keeping First Things First

One day a friend dropped by Chuck Swindoll's office with "a word" for him. He said, "I'm concerned that as you get busier, your time with God and the study of the scriptures will become less and less important. Don't let that happen!" That's a word we all need!

As the early church grew, the demand on the Apostles became greater. Realizing that the urgent was about to overtake the important, they said, "Look ye out among you seven men… whom we may appoint over this business. But we will give ourselves continually to prayer and to the ministry of the word" (Acts 6:3-7 KJV).

After reading this, I made six promises to myself. Here they are:

(1)   I promise to work hard, study, and try to stay fresh; those who read what I write deserve no less.

(2)   I promise to maintain a heart for God; to pray fervently and frequently, and stay devoted to my Lord and to my calling.

(3)   I promise to be accountable. I've learned that living the life of a lone-ranger is too dangerous.

(4)   I promise to stay faithful to my family; my wife, my children, and my grandchildren deserve my time and my undivided affection.

(5)   I promise to be who I am - just me; to keep comforting the afflicted, and afflicting the comfortable.

(6)   I promise to accept each day as a gift, live it to the max, and become all that God intended me to be!

In other words, I plan to keep trying to put first things first!
How about you?

A Healthy Attitude Toward Yourself

If you want to develop a healthy attitude toward yourself, you need to regularly confess these 12 things:

1. I know God created me and that He loves me (Jer 31:3).
2. I have shortcomings and I want to change. I believe that God is working in my life each day; while He is, I can still accept and enjoy myself.
3. Everyone has faults; I am not a failure because I'm not perfect.
4. I'm working with God to overcome my faults, but there'll always be something to work on; therefore I won't be discouraged when He convicts me of areas that need improvement.
5. I want people to like me, but my sense of worth is not dependent on them. Jesus has already demonstrated my worth by dying for me.
6. I won't be controlled by what others think, say, or do. If they reject me, I'll survive, for God has promised never to reject me as long as I keep believing.
7. No matter how often I fail I won't give up, because God is with me. He has promised to strengthen and sustain me as long as I live (Heb 13:5).
8. I like myself; I don't like everything I do, and I want to change – but I refuse to put myself down.
9. I am acceptable to God through the blood of Jesus (Eph 2:8-9).
10. God has a plan for my life and I'm going to fulfill it; I have God-given gifts and I intend to use them to glorify Him.
11. In myself I am nothing, but in Christ I am everything I need to be.
12. I can do whatever God calls me to do, through the power of Him who dwells in me. (Php 4:13).

Lighten Up!

Most of us are far too serious. We're uptight about everything; being five minutes late, getting stuck in traffic, somebody giving us a wrong look, waiting in line, over-cooking a meal, gaining a pound, discovering a wrinkle, making an honest mistake; you name it - we lose all perspective over it! The problem is – we have unrealistic expectations!

If you want to experience the joy God's promised you, do these 2 things: (1) admit that your uptightness is largely because of the way you have decided life should be and (2) understand that your expectations are causing your frustrations. If you keep expecting things to always be a certain way and they aren't, then you'll always be upset.

Here's an idea: try approaching your life today without all those expectations. For example, don't require everybody to be friendly, then when some are, you'll be delighted. Don't expect your day to be trouble-free; instead when problems come up, just say, "Thank you Lord for another chance to grow." Go ahead, do it and you'll see how much better everything is. Rather than fighting against life, you'll be flowing with it. Pretty soon, if you work at it, you'll enjoy your life more, and other people will enjoy being around you much more too!

Change How You Think

You don't have more problems than other people – you just think about them more often! It's what you think that produces how you feel. If you don't believe that, try getting angry without first having angry thoughts, or sad without having sad thoughts. You can't do it! To experience a feeling, you must first have the thought that produces it!

So what can you do? Change how you think and you'll change how you feel. Nothing can hold your negative feelings in place other than your own thinking. The next time you're feeling upset, notice your thinking – it'll be negative. It's always that way.

The truth is, it's your thinking that is negative, not your life! Once you understand that, you're back on the path toward happiness again.

But change takes time; you didn't become negative overnight and you won't become positive overnight. You can start by treating your negative thoughts in the same way you'd treat flies at a picnic – just shoo them away and replace them with thoughts that are "excellent or praiseworthy." Why? Because when you change how you think, you'll change how you feel!

Free From The Opinions Of People

If you let it, criticism will steal your individuality, rob you of your creativity and stop you from fulfilling your destiny. Insecure people will always criticize you if your choices are different from theirs. Why? Because they're uncomfortable with things that don't conform to their way of thinking.

On the other hand, secure people can handle "being the only one" doing something. They can allow others the liberty to be different and to make their own choices. Why? Because they're secure in who they are.

Jesus made "himself of no reputation" (Php 2:7). He obviously wasn't too concerned about what others thought of Him. He had a goal – to do the Father's will – no more and no less. He also knew that to do it, He had to be free from the opinions of others!

To me the greatest tragedy in life would be to grow old, and know that somewhere along the way I had "lost myself" and never succeeded at being who God called me to be. Paul says it this way: "It matters very little to me what you think of me, even less where I rank in popular opinion. I don't even rank myself... the Master makes that judgment" (1Co 4: 3-4 TM). That is an example worth copying!

Others May Not Notice, But God Does

"Thank you!" Two simple words, but oh how much they mean. Has it been a while since you heard them? You do so much for so many, now you just want a little appreciation in return.

Others may neglect to thank you, but know this - your heavenly Father appreciates you for all you do, and all you are. He has put you exactly where He needs you and you are fulfilling His purpose every day!

When you understand that, you'll begin to find meaning in everything you do. He is the reason – others are just the beneficiaries!

Don't let somebody else's response decide the level of your joy! They may not notice, but God does. He records and He rewards. Count on it!

If you feel unappreciated today, stop and read these words carefully: "Whatever you do, whether in word or deed, do it all in the name of the Lord…" (Col 3:17 NIV). That's it - do it for Him!

Why don't you pray this prayer: "Lord, all that I do today, I do for you. I know that you appreciate me – look at all the gifts that you have given me. In return, I will praise and honor you throughout this day by my thoughts, my words, and my actions. Amen."

Chapter Nine

Able To Marshal And Direct
Our Energies Wisely

Pursue Excellence

Listen carefully to these words: "Excellence requires 100% all the time. If you doubt that, try maintaining excellence by setting your standards at 92% or even 95%. Pretty soon you'll figure you're doing fine so long as you get somewhere near it. When that happens, excellence gets reduced to acceptable, and before long acceptable doesn't seem worth the sweat if you can get by with adequate. After that - mediocrity is only a breath away."

Paul described his goal as "the high calling" (Php 3:14). That means if you want to reach it, you've got to aim high every day! Paul added, "I strain to reach the end of the race and receive the prize" (Php 3:14 LB). You've got to choose excellence, and be willing to pay the price to achieve it.

In a recent survey of very successful people, it was found that most of them failed an average of seven times before they succeeded. That means the more you try, the more failure you'll experience, and the more success you'll enjoy. You can't have one without the other.

John Maxwell says, "I'd rather reach ninety percent of my potential with plenty of mistakes, than only ten percent with a perfect score. Each time you run the race and fail to finish first, examine your progress. Success is coming third out of four, and being excited because you came fifth last time." If you've been settling for less, reconsider, refocus, and recommit yourself to excellence.

Whatever It Costs – It Costs

Success is usually given only at the end of great struggle! If it came easy, everybody would have it. That's why a lot of us procrastinate, hoping we can find an easier way. But it doesn't work! Whatever it costs – it costs; there are no swapping price tags! The value of anything is determined by the price you pay for it. Furthermore, you won't easily jeopardize something when you remember what it cost you.

What are you afraid of anyway? Failing? Your greatest concern should be the opposite - regret that you didn't even try. Are you afraid of criticism? Face it, as you move upwards certain people will find your success offensive, whether you're arrogant or not. If they do, that's their problem - unless you make it yours by getting insecure or defensive.

We all want to be liked, but at some point you've got to ask yourself, "How much am I willing to lose in order to be accepted?" Nehemiah cried, "I am doing a great work, so that I cannot come down" (Ne 6:3). Anytime you defer to the opinions of people, instead the will of God, you are "coming down."

Advancement often brings isolation and criticism - and God may be grooming you right now for a new level of blessing by exposing you to both. Can you handle it? Not everybody can! But if you're the kind of person who can't sit on the bleachers while others play the game – then go for it! God will reward every step of faith, and every sacrifice you make!

Drifting or Purpose-Driven?

Purpose-driven people will always leave their safety zone, and go where the fearful won't. Things that cause others to break down only cause them to break through - and even break records. If you want what you've never had, you must be willing to go where you've never gone.

Purpose-driven people will always walk alone because they see what others don't! Look at Elijah - one man against 850 prophets. But he prevailed! When David killed Goliath everybody wanted to be his friend, but when he went out to face the giant - he went alone. So what's new?

Purpose-driven people know how to deal with temptation! It's worthy of note that Joseph faced more temptation in a palace than he ever did in a prison, and it was only when David left the battlefield that he got into trouble with Bathsheba. Do you know the time and the area of your greatest vulnerability? What are you doing to protect yourself?

Purpose-driven people "never arrive!" They know that satisfaction is the enemy of success. To those who said, "I am rich and increased with goods and have need of nothing," God replied, "I will spew thee out of my mouth" (Rev 3:16). Never stop learning! Never stop growing! Never stop reaching!

Clinton Utterbach has a wonderful sign in his office that reads - "Those who walk with God always reach their destination!" That just about says it all, doesn't it?

When Things Go Wrong

The world is not going to devote itself to making you happy! Only when you accept that can you begin to move forward. Life doesn't always work the way you want it to. Paul wrote, "Whensoever I take my journey into Spain, I will come to you..." (Ro 15:24). But he never got there; instead, he landed in one of the worst prisons in Europe. But from there, he wrote the epistles.

Look out! Your disappointment may turn out to be - God's appointment. The Bible says, "In his heart a man plans his course, but the Lord determines his steps" (Pr 16:9 NIV). Aren't you glad He's in control of your life? Let the philosophers argue over why life works as it does; just focus on how to live it! If you live to be a hundred, what good is it if resentment and regret keep you from enjoying a day of it? And what good is more time if you're only killing the time you've got?

Remember how an oyster makes a pearl? When a grain of sand gets into its shell and irritates it, instead of resisting and resenting it, the oyster wraps it in layer after layer of beauty until a pearl if formed. The poet said, "Now this tale has a moral for isn't it grand what an oyster can do with a morsel of sand; what couldn't we do if we'd only begin with some of the things that get under our skin?" God is working in everything you're going through today, for your good and His glory. All you need to do is trust Him.

Are You Struggling With Change?

You'll miss what God's planning for you next if you worship the past and yearn for yesterday. If you've ever lost a loved one, you know what I'm talking about. Death wrenches from us those we'd cling to forever. But we can't, for death is a part of life. We make peace with it only when we realize that it's a door that enables our loved ones to move from a lesser to a greater realm of existence.

Parents, don't try to live your life a second time through your children. Keep your mind fresh by having expectations that go beyond the goals you have for them. Don't try to cling on to a relationship that's changed because you "need to be needed." When Samuel the prophet was born, his mother Hannah said, "...I will give him unto the Lord all the days of his life..." (1Sa 1:11).

It's easier to give them back when you understand they are not yours to keep. Be grateful for the gift of children and the satisfaction of a job well done, then ask, "What's next?"

If you recognize areas in your life where you've been guilty of resisting change, allow God to cleanse your heart from the fear. Something good is going to come out of it. God doesn't change - but His methods of ministering to you will change over and over again. He may not bring you the same way twice, but "goodness and mercy" will follow you all the days of your life (Ps 23:6). What more could you ask for?

Be Patient

If God has promised you a certain thing, wait on it, for His promise will surely come to pass. Just because it hasn't happened yet doesn't mean God's changed His mind. The timing may not be right for Him to get the ultimate glory and you to get the ultimate benefit.

We are to "let patience have her perfect work, that ye may be perfect and entire, wanting nothing" (Jas 1:4). Waiting can be a passive posture, but patience is an active principle, because those "through faith and patience inherit the promises" (Heb 6:12). You say, "How long will I have to wait?" Probably longer than you want to! It's all about learning patience. God set His watch to accomplish His purpose, not yours. After all, "We know that all things work... according to His purpose" (Ro 8:28).

When you know His purpose, you won't permit things that are contrary to it. You'll know how to allocate your time, your effort, and your money - where you can go, and where not to go.

God says, "I make known the end from the beginning..." (Isa 46:10 NIV). First He establishes the purpose, then He determines the procedure. So what do you do while you're waiting? We should rejoice in the Lord and in our salvation, "even though the olive crop fails, and the fields lie empty and barren" (Hab 3:17-18 NLT). Begin praising the Lord today for what He's going to do for you - because He absolutely will come through for you!

The Power Of A Goal

Fifty percent of the people you know don't know where they're going. Another 40% will go in any direction they're led. The remaining 10% know where they'd like to go - but less than half of them ever pay the price to get there. One day Oliver Wendell Holmes lost his train ticket. As he searched for it, obviously irritated, the conductor told him, "It's ok your Honor, just mail it in. We all know you and trust you." Holmes replied, "Sir, I'm not worried about finding my ticket - I just want to know where I'm going!"

Goals are what make it possible for you to know where you're going. Jesus could endure the shame of the cross, because He saw the glory of the resurrection, and the birth of a church that would change the world. Moses could give up the comforts of a palace, because he saw the Promised Land.

J.C. Penney said, "Give me a stock clerk with a goal, and I'll give you a man who'll make history. On the other hand, give me a man without a goal, and I'll give you a stock clerk." You see, while you work on your goals, your goals are working on you, and what you get by reaching them is not nearly as important as what you become along the way!

What are your goals today? Are they clear enough to write down? Short enough to fit into a paragraph? Strong enough to help you persevere? Valuable enough to make you pay the price? If they are, you'll see them fulfilled!

Get Back To Prayer

You'll learn more in an hour with God than you'll learn in a lifetime with anybody else. The enemy knows what your God-given potential is, and he's out to stop you before you get there. Prayer puts a shield of divine protection over you! (Don't be without it!)

There are people you know who won't be around next year unless someone prays for them. There are many who thought that they, of all people, would never cheat on their taxes, or their partner, but they did. Unless you acknowledge the propensity for sin that's within you, you won't pray against it, and you'll always be vulnerable to the enemy's attack.

Jesus said, "Stay alert; be in prayer, so you won't wander into temptation without even knowing you're in danger. There's a part of you that is eager, ready for anything in God. But there's another part that's as lazy as an old dog sleeping by the fire" (Mt 26:41 TM). Could the language be clearer?

The most lethal weapon the enemy has against you is - you! That's right; your old carnal sin nature must be taken daily to the cross and crucified. The place of prayer is where you do that. In God's presence see yourself as He sees you. There, at the point of repentance, He reveals, He removes, and He restores. When your prayer life goes, so does your protection. So get busy and do something about it.